The Ethics of Lacanian Psychoanalysis

The Ethics of Lacanian Psychoanalysis observes different aspects of life – childhood, romantic love, sex, death, and human suffering – through a Lacanian lens, with a glance toward a Buddhist point of view.

Combining Lacanian psychoanalysis with insight from Freud, Bion, and the Zen masters, this book suggests finding ways to suffer less and cultivate a passion for life. Yehuda Israely and Esther Pelled consider the ethics in the light of which people live, and the questions pertinent to this choice. What kind of person do you want to be? What desire will you choose your life to be led by? How will you deal with separations, relationships, and cravings that you cannot control? This book raises these questions and proposes possible answers through an accessible, conversational format.

The Ethics of Lacanian Psychoanalysis will be of interest to psychoanalysts in practice and in training as well as readers looking to learn more about applying Lacanian ideas to everyday life.

Yehuda Israely, Ph.D., is a psychologist, psychoanalyst, and writer. He is the winner of the 2011 Geffen award for original sci-fi literature. He is a Founding member of the Forum Lacan Tel-Aviv and a member of The International Forums of the Lacanian Field.

Esther Pelled, Ph.D., is a psychologist and writer. She was awarded the Sapir Prize for literature in 2017. Her doctorate dealt with a comparative study of Buddhist thought and psychoanalysis.

T0384881

The Ethics of Lacanian Psychoanalysis

A Conversation about Living in Joy

Yehuda Israely and Esther Pelled

Translated from the Hebrew by Yardenne Greenspan

Routledge
Taylor & Francis Group

LONDON AND NEW YORK

Designed cover image: Cover image © Yehuda Israely

First published 2023
by Routledge
4 Park Square, Milton Park, Abingdon, Oxon OX14 4RN

and by Routledge
605 Third Avenue, New York, NY 10158

Routledge is an imprint of the Taylor & Francis Group, an informa business

British Library Cataloguing-in-Publication Data
A catalogue record for this book is available from the British Library

ISBN: 978-1-032-37893-0 (hbk)
ISBN: 978-1-032-37891-6 (pbk)
ISBN: 978-1-003-34245-8 (ebk)

DOI: 10.4324/9781003342458

Typeset in Times New Roman
by Apex, CoVantage, LLC

We wish to thank Shira and Daniel Pelled

Contents

Chapter 1

The Human Condition – and in Light of It

Psychoanalysis as Ethics

In this chapter we will offer some postulations of Lacanian psychoanalysis: about man as chooser, about human choice as independent from outside forces, and the derivative: the human condition of orphanhood (with no one to explain the right way to live) – orphanhood as the opposite of isolation, and the switch from "the correct way to live" to "the preferable way to live."

ESTHER: So what is this book, Yehuda? And what is it about?

YEHUDA: This book is about what people can attain for themselves, for their lives, and mental health. This book is about the possibility of living better with one-self and one's surroundings, and of fulfilling desires. It's possible for people to benefit from Lacanian wisdom not only through treatment. What we're doing right now is an unconventional, controversial act.

ESTHER: Why?

YEHUDA: The personal relationship between psychoanalyst and patient bears knowledge. A book, on the other hand, cannot be part of an interpersonal relationship, cannot be a partner in transference. The benefit of one-on-one psychoanalysis is immense. It is the kitchen where ethics are prepared, and it is user-unique. I myself owe a lot to this practice and am not familiar with any worthy substitute. Nevertheless, I've often come across situations in my personal as well as my professional life, in which reading a piece of writing has changed my life. The written word can open people up to new ideas, and reading can therefore be a formative experience in spite of the lack of trans-ference found in a clinician's office. A fertilizing, life-changing relationship can occur between a person and a text.

ESTHER: Indeed.

YEHUDA: Reading can create understanding, or an even deeper change. Therefore, the question is, can we write Lacanian wisdom into a book that a person can benefit from reading? This is the purpose of this book.

ESTHER: Let's begin, then, from your suggestion – offering people a different way to look at their lives, another tool through which to understand themselves and steer their lives through this understanding. If this is the purpose of our work together, what should be the concept at the center of this book?

DOI: 10.4324/9781003342458-1

YEHUDA: I don't know what concept is at the center of this book. I do know what should be the first concept we introduce. The opening concept is "ethics." The study of ethics revolves around the question of the right way to live. Jewish ethics claims that the right way to live involves adhering to the mitzvahs. Buddhist ethics argues that one must find freedom from suffering through freedom from the desire which causes the suffering. There are different schools of knowledge, some of them spiritual. Other schools, such as secular liberalism, psychoanalysis in general or Lacanian psychoanalysis specifically, carry no spiritual pretense. They deal with understanding the psyche and share an ethical orientation: offering guidance to people with regards to the question of how one ought to live.

ESTHER: This is the place to mention that the ethical aspect is common both to "spiritual" schools – those that are connected to religious faith – and "mental" schools. Both include basic assumptions regarding the question of how one ought to live. I'm pointing this out specifically because subscribers to "mental" schools of thought are not fans of this comparison between them and subscribers to "spiritual" schools of thought. Nevertheless, in this aspect, they have a lot in common.

YEHUDA: Indeed, they share the ethical aspect. And yet, the answer to this question can differ widely across schools of thought, and the difference stems from the axiom of each such school regarding the structure of the mind and its principles of action. Lacanian psychoanalysis is traditionally embarrassed about the question of ethics.

ESTHER: Why is that?

YEHUDA: On the surface, it denounces the idea of telling people how to live. There is a paradox around the question of ethics: on the one hand, the meaning of ethics is answering the question of how one ought to live. On the other hand, a central principle of psychoanalytic ethics is that each person can make their own decisions regarding their values, their desires, and the way in which to manage the relationship between the two. Therefore, the first item in this guidance must be: The decision of how to live is given to each person. Each of us must decide for ourselves.

ESTHER: This first principle, according to which each person decides for themselves, raises a question: Do individuals make their own decisions freely, without any limitations? Are there no outer boundaries to their choice?

YEHUDA: Of course, there are limitations. They are the limitations deduced from the cards people have drawn in life. Paradoxically, one of these cards represents the measure of freedom the person believes they have, or, more generally, belief in freedom of choice. People's reasoning and preferences have been enforced before they are born, but when they wish to change them, or, alternatively, when they wish to accept their natural inclinations – they can be more liberated. The more they realize how unfree they are, how bound to the conscious and unconscious influences that have molded their lives, how affected by the words and desires of those around them and of previous generations, the more they can choose to set themselves free, and ultimately to accept the limits of this freedom, meaning – acknowledging what can and what cannot be changed. This is the analytic process.

ESTHER: In this way, you place the subject alone at the center of the universe, and if I'm understanding you correctly, this is a universe without a sky. The subject, if they so wish, can choose their own sky – a faith in a greater power. But you leave this choice to them. So is this the human condition? Each of us is totally alone.

YEHUDA: Not exactly.

ESTHER: How's that?

YEHUDA: Not alone. Because we are already laden with values, with history. And also: individuals are not distinct from their surroundings, but embedded within them. And yet, there are positions from which they alone can choose.

ESTHER: In other words, while I fear that an individual alone cannot stand the task of deciding for their own lives, and I rush to their aid, adding boundaries, and in extreme cases even divine boundaries, you are telling me that individuals suffer from an abundance, not a shortage of tools and advisors helping them shape their lives. Meaning, your basic assumption regarding the apparatus of human consciousness is in opposition to mine!

YEHUDA: Indeed. They suffer from a surplus of identifications.

ESTHER: Oh dear, Yehuda. How is it that as soon as we started talking, we spiraled into a philosophical discussion? I'm saying this because you began with a postmodern statement. If man alone makes the choice, and there are no external boundaries (or, in another world, there is nothing transcendental around him) then our starting-off point involves no statements regarding absolute good or absolute evil. There is no moral starting-off point whatsoever.

YEHUDA: Correct. We are born into a given reality – social, symbolic, and moral. That is our apparatus. There is no exterior authority determining criteria of what we ought to want or choose. Of course, some believe that astrologers can elucidate the directives of the stars, and we are each born into a country in which the legislators' interests have passed certain laws rather than others, but this is not psychoanalytic ethics. In psychoanalysis, we wish to reveal the desire behind the order, thus dismantling its control.

ESTHER: So, what you're saying is – not to worry, there will be many people and entities "assisting" with the choice. There is an entire supermarket of spiritual and mental options –

YEHUDA: No, that's not what I meant. I'm saying we are all preloaded with values, directions, and ideals that we are born into, and which we can, to a certain extent, shed.

ESTHER: Born into . . . should we refer to these as "the superego"?

YEHUDA: No. Part of what we ought to understand about life is that we can't always liberate ourselves from these values, nor should we. The fantasy of being free of influence is something to be addressed. There is no such state of freedom from internalization.

ESTHER: The ambition to be free from influence is obsessive . . . But that isn't what I was getting at. On the contrary: I'm referring to the experience of loneliness implied by your statements. The loneliness of a subject who must decide on their own.

YEHUDA: In that case, I wouldn't call it loneliness. Rather, orphanhood. Loneliness is a state of having no friends. Orphanhood is the state of having no parents.

ESTHER: Okay, yes, they must choose without help from their parents . . .

YEHUDA: Without parents, meaning without authorities dictating their choice. Without someone choosing criteria for them.

ESTHER: And so, ultimately, without a superego.

YEHUDA: That's why even this book cannot make statements about right and wrong; the only statement that can be asserted is that people will decide for themselves, which already entails desire as a value.

ESTHER: I'll speak a little about my impressions so far. In spite of the attempt to avoid the absolute nature of "right," I find a dimension of hermetic and excessive certainty in your position. Though you are representing a postmodern stance, a stance avoiding statements of a single truth, a certainty about what is "right," you are making statements of certainty about what is "preferable." See? There is no statement about what is right, but there is a statement about what is preferable. As for me, the difference between the right and the preferable isn't entirely clear to me. You're saying: there is no absolute truth, we each choose our own truth, the truth of our desire. There is definitely an unequivocal stance regarding the preferable.

YEHUDA: Yes, there are things I define as preferable.

ESTHER: You talk about absolute freedom in the ideological sense of your proposal; because "preferable" means there is no necessity, no obvious choice, no one thing that is better than another. And that's something I find hard to believe.

YEHUDA: Then let me be more specific: a law – the signifier of "good" or "right" – is a result of somebody's interest, and therefore does not represent absolute truth.

ESTHER: Let's examine this idea through the extreme case of sociopathy, a mental disorder characterized, say, by a lack of conscience.

YEHUDA: A sociopath is someone not subjected to others' interests. He has no law. And yet far be it from me to judge him. I just need to be careful of him.

ESTHER: Meaning, you have no moral stance on psychopathy – it is neither good nor bad in your eyes – just as you have no moral stance regarding any other mental condition. Or perhaps it would be more accurate to say: it is a choice as any other.

YEHUDA: Correct.

ESTHER: It is quite a demand of yourself, as a psychoanalyst, to be without a moral stance.

YEHUDA: Yes.

ESTHER: It is a demand I doubt you can meet.

YEHUDA: True, I often don't.

ESTHER: The demand to condemn nothing, to prefer nothing over anything else.

YEHUDA: I often fail.

ESTHER: Okay. What does that mean?

YEHUDA: I have my own subjective limitations of how much I can meet my own ethics. But I still adhere to it, even if I don't meet it.

ESTHER: Is this ethics a kind of absolute?

YEHUDA: Yes. It's ethics that views laws as fiction. For example, when it comes to teaching children to be lawful, I am in favor of lying to them and telling them there is such thing as the law, then, at some point, confessing the lie in order to set them free.

ESTHER: Yes, bringing them up to respect the law but later to have the freedom to either choose it or reject it.

YEHUDA: Even when I feel revulsion regarding the sociopath or his way of life, it's a kind of lie that infects me as well. Meaning, I feel my own revulsion, and yet I reject this revulsion. For instance: to some vegans, meat eaters are sociopaths, while some gastronomists consider vegans to be misanthropes. There is no single, righteous, objective community that determines who is in the right. When a mafia goon refuses to follow an order, are they following the law or breaking it? That depends on their frame of reference, and the choice is theirs. Is a freedom fighter in a country run by a dictator an outlaw? Depending on whose law. In their eyes, they did not appoint the judge to judge them.

ESTHER: So what this means, actually, is that the entire social-moral institution is founded on a fictitious entity.

YEHUDA: That is the imaginary big, Other, with a capital O. And the Lacanian idea is: the Other doesn't exist, but that is no reason to reject it, because it is essential.

ESTHER: So it's useful.

YEHUDA: Yes.

ESTHER: Meaning, you've reduced ideas of "right" and "good" that have existed from the dawn of humankind, to the "useful."

YEHUDA: Right. I'm descending from heaven to earth, and what exists down here is usefulness and desire. Because even faith in the law should be seen as a cause of desire. Desire was first born in individuals as an effect of the law that sets limits on indulgence. That is the formative Oedipus complex.

ESTHER: How does faith in the law serve desire?

YEHUDA: My personal trainer orders me to do exercises that I really don't feel like doing, but I'm paying her to tyrannize me, to achieve my goals even when I don't feel like working for them. Meaning, I am recruiting her as a representative of the law.

ESTHER: So ultimately desire is also the master of the law?

YEHUDA: Yes. Exactly. And even if the law is originally the parent of desire, desire can make use of it. In the family oedipal myth, it's the law of the father

who stands between the child and the mother, causing identification with the
father and his desire. This identification supports desire.

ESTHER: I think there's another necessary factor: there is desire, and there is law
that is governed by desire.

YEHUDA: And there's excess *jouissance*, Lacan's term for pleasure-pain-
excitement-over indulgence, meaning, desire uses the law to restrain *jouissance*, because *jouissance* doesn't allow desire.

ESTHER: "*Jouissance*" is the psychological aspect of acting "outside of the law."
Like obesity, for instance?

YEHUDA: Any symptom. Obesity, addiction . . .

ESTHER: Does *jouissance* come at the expense of desire?

YEHUDA: The law exists in order to restrain and, paradoxically, produce desire.
Saying that it is intended for this purpose means attributing intention to it,
which is not the case. In the case of the personal trainer, there is an intention
of using the law in order to produce desire. But parents often restrain their
children out of an intention to prevent indulgence, not realizing they are pro-
ducing desire.

ESTHER: Okay.

YEHUDA: "Indulgence" is a relevant concept for all addictions and symptoms.
Sometimes, depression is a kind of an addiction too, it can be seen as a kind
of submission to indulgence.

ESTHER: I'd like to circle back to ethics and the question of how to live. Back
in the day, when we started discussing this book, you spoke about ethics in
terms of our lives with others – as parents or part of a couple. You used the
term "psychoanalytic ethics." There are Jewish ethics, Buddhist ethics, and
liberal ethics – and this paradigm we're discussing here – psychoanalysis –
offers its own form. Its own answer to the question of how to live.

YEHUDA: This is my own personal perception: that this can be implemented as a
way of life, and not only at the clinician's office.

ESTHER: Meaning, there are areas of Lacanian thought that you identify as directly
actualized in your own life as a person, not an analyst.

YEHUDA: Yes indeed.

ESTHER: Can you give me an example that's relevant to this book? Divorce, parenting, discipline . . .

YEHUDA: I'll offer an example from adolescence. A teenager who rebels seems,
at first, to simply rebel against authority. But a deeper look reveals them
to be provoking authority into action, out of a refusal to become orphaned.
According to the first approach – "rebelling against authority" – the parents'
response would be to force their rules on the teenager, and the result would
be the teenager continuing to reinforce authority through further provocation.

ESTHER: Why? If he gets hit over the head, why should he stick out his neck again?

YEHUDA: Because deep down he knows it cannot hold. He knows that, in truth,
there is no authority. He is exactly in the phase of realizing there is no authority, and this truth frightens him. So, he or she takes all sorts of action to make

sure they won't be abandoned or orphaned, to ensure someone will try to control them.

ESTHER: In that case, the deeper motivation to continue to rebel is that even though he or she has received a response – a punishment or a rebuke – they cannot accept it. They cannot accept the parental response, because she or he knows it isn't real, that there is no true power behind it.

YEHUDA: It won't take. Its effect will last a very short time before fizzling out. The sense that someone is protecting them from themselves will fizzle out. So, the teenager will search for his master through further provocation. The alternative for a parent who believes in authority is getting upset about their helplessness with the child. Helpless as opposed to what they believe they ought to be: a parental authority.

On the other hand, the parent who subscribes to the Lacanian approach would be compassionate toward the child, because this child, as they grow up, will find out the painful truth – that there is nobody to conduct their life for them. So they will tell the child: Look, I'm helpless. I'm helpless because you are your own manager. But they, the parents, won't be depressed, won't be too critical of themselves, won't see themselves as failures. And the child would receive lots of love, but not the illusion that they are dismissed from making a choice. More than that: they will realize that they themselves have to choose.

ESTHER: So actually, in a way, you aspire – aspire, simple as that – for the moment when your child realizes that the person standing before them, their father, is their partner, rather than their ruler.

YEHUDA: Not even a partner.

ESTHER: A partner in the sense that their father loves them and cares about them, but not someone who can decide how they should live.

YEHUDA: I wouldn't call that a partner. A partner is someone who's signed an agreement. That's the relationship I have with my patients.

ESTHER: So how shall we position you in conjunction with your child? What word shall we use?

YEHUDA: I love him, I'm his parent, but not in the authoritative sense. If you want to use the word partner, then I'm his partner in solidarity with regard to the lack of authority.

ESTHER: It's as if you're extracting from the words "father" and "mother" something that is typically included in them according to most human consciousness.

YEHUDA: I'm not rejecting the signifiers "father" and "mother." They contain an irreplaceable emotional charge that would be a shame to give up, but I am enabling a sobering from the authority we attribute to them. In an age-appropriate way, of course. Another vital factor in understanding this picture: culture. In some cultures, parents' word remains law throughout their off-spring's lives. They are the heads of the clan. Other cultures are more like ours – in adolescence parents are dismissed from their roles as representatives of the law. But I'm referring to a situation in which the parent will-fully resigns from the role. Meaning: youthful rebellion is unnecessary and depends on the parent's position in relation to the teenager. The more the parent pretends to be the law, the more rebellion they have to suffer through. The more authoritative the parent, the more they answer the child's unconscious wish to avoid being orphaned.

ESTHER: Denying orphanhood; I'm repeating the sequence of relations to this central term: a teenager is a child shedding their innocence, already suspecting that their parents are not truly the law's representatives. They are startled by this suspicion and attempt to return and verify the equation: parents = the law. That's why they rebel. The reason they panic is that acknowledging that parents aren't the law and cannot enforce the law leads teenagers to feel that they are, in truth, all alone, masters of their own lives, and in this sense, they are orphans. Orphaned of the law. And they don't want to know that, so they rebel, to arouse their parents' urge to function as lawmen.

Now I'd like to linger on this expression, orphanhood. To me, this is the main thing. You position humans as the ultimate decision makers in their lives. They make these decisions all alone.

YEHUDA: Not all alone, but without protection.

ESTHER: They are orphans.

YEHUDA: Being an orphan doesn't mean being alone. In fact, the orphan is much more connected to people because he is free to choose the connections he wants.

ESTHER: Yes, that's right, but this word "choice," you know, brings up inevitable connotations of death that cannot be ignored.

YEHUDA: It is a death. The death of authority. The parents don't have to die for the authority to die.

ESTHER: When you present being an orphan in this way, it seems like a desirable position to be in, because you're using the term to signify freedom.

YEHUDA: That's right.

ESTHER: So it becomes a happy idea. But I'd like to remind you that for most people, when we're reminded of orphanhood and death, we become sullen.

YEHUDA: Because there's something sad about it.

ESTHER: Okay, so let's take a look at the dialectics. Let's look at this transaction from both sides. Yes, the sad part is sobering from the illusion of being protected.

YEHUDA: Right, sobering from protection.

ESTHER: And in that sense, God is like a parent. A "personal providence" kind of God.

YEHUDA: Correct.

ESTHER: Okay, so there's no personal protection.

YEHUDA: Exactly, exactly.

ESTHER: Got it. No personal protection. But if that's the case, you can't assume the world is necessarily aspiring to good. If we kill God, we necessarily give up the illusion of aspiring to good that connects people together. Am I wrong?

YEHUDA: I'll give you an example from a patient of mine whose partner infected him with HIV. He came in to treat his depression. When I asked him if anyone ever promised him that this kind of thing would never happen, he admitted that nobody ever promised him that, and his depression lifted. Meaning, he was living like a person who was meant to be protected but wasn't, until he realized he was never meant to be protected, and so no promise had been broken. There's a tragedy, but not a betrayal.

ESTHER: Did his boyfriend know he was sick when he slept with your patient? That could answer my question about assuming goodness.

YEHUDA: The patient's anger wasn't at his partner, who may have cheated him by not disclosing the truth; it was at the world, for not delivering what he thought had been promised at a much younger age, before people can wake up from the fantasy of entitlement.

ESTHER: Why me, why did this happen to me, of all people.

YEHUDA: Yes, yes. That relates to your question, about whether there is a human camaraderie focused on the good. He believed there was, and when he discovered there hadn't been, he felt betrayed. I helped him figure out that this was never promised to him. Even if he had parents who wanted the best for him, that didn't mean there is a God, or a social contract that promises goods. At least not in the sense of promise and protection.

ESTHER: This is a personal case and it's a disaster, but it isn't about a broken promise, because there never had been one. Is that what you're saying?

YEHUDA: Yes.

ESTHER: Meaning, there is no generalization, not even about an aspiration for good that connects humans on earth. No generalization.

YEHUDA: Correct. And this enables some freedom from narcissism.

ESTHER: How?

YEHUDA: Because in the case of narcissism, the assumption is that my parents should have made things work out for me, and when they don't I take it personally, blaming them for failing at their job, even though if they did have trouble giving me what I needed – either because of their life circumstances or their personal limitations – there's no point in taking it personally. In this sense, the idea of personal protection contains a narcissistic element: I am the center of the world, God sees me and protects me. The narcissistic stance – of assuming the existence of personal protection – is passive, while the orphan actively works to make his wishes come true, including the wish not to be alone.

ESTHER: And yet, as soon as you are left alone – like we did today – and you have freedom of choice, you are an orphan, and you can choose your own faith, meaning you can –

YEHUDA: I can pay a personal trainer.

ESTHER: Or you can simply be good, aspire to good, even if this aspiration isn't universal. In other words, your "religiosity," or your moral stance, becomes unconditional and independent from big or small influences, it is not reactive but self-standing. Just as you are alone in your every decision, you make an independent choice to be good. Not because that's how you were brought up, not because it's the law, meaning, it's the way things should be done, and not because that's what everybody does, but because you want to.

YEHUDA: And yet, psychoanalytic ethics assumes that if you follow your wishes, you will be doing good.

ESTHER: Yes, what should we do about that? I mean, where did that assumption come from?

YEHUDA: From the fact that the subject – the willful entity – is a social creature.

ESTHER: Is that the idea of "the desire of the other?"

YEHUDA: Yes. The desire is transferred from the other through language, that's why you must be a socially embedded creature. An individual in society is like a word in a sentence. That's why desire isn't something you can do at the expense of your surrounding; desire that goes against its surroundings is ego, is separateness. Psychoanalytic ethics isn't aimed at the ego. The subject, meaning, the wanter, is socially embedded.

ESTHER: Socially embedded because they exist by virtue of being within a society rather than existing independently?

YEHUDA: Look, to fulfil the desire for a certain profession, you must be part of a context of professions and social needs.

ESTHER: To become a gardener, there need to be gardens and for people to care about aesthetics.

YEHUDA: You must be a member of your organization. You must play a part in creating an organization that offers you a place as a subject. In that sense, you are acting for the benefit of society, so you can settle into this society. If you aren't, you can't have desires.

ESTHER: This is the Buddhist theory of dependent origination. The theory discusses apartness as an illusion of independent existence. The illusion of separateness is referred to in Buddhism as "I" and in Lacanian Theory as "Imaginary." Meaning, the way you wish to appear in your own eyes rather than who you truly are. In truth, you are a psychoanalyst because you have patients, and a writer because you have readers. All of your aspects are other-dependent. That's why you can never be independent. In order to be something in this world, you require the world. You need your son in order to be his father and your wife in order to be her husband. As soon as you realize this, you agree to be dependent, agree to an interdependent relationship. Then, and only then, can you truly live, because you can be something for someone, and they can be something for you. In many ways, almost across all theories, this is precisely the opposite of narcissism. Not being a narcissist means looking in the mirror and seeing not only yourself, but everyone around you, in the reflection. See what I did there?

YEHUDA: The mirror metaphor is confusing because it belongs to narcissism.

ESTHER: Of course, I know that. And yet, when you see yourself, you must see your father, your mother, your children, your patients, your friends, your readers, and those who wrote about the same subjects before you as well. That's what I mean. Acknowledge the fact that you can't do it without them and shouldn't be able to.

YEHUDA: Right. And this is where I'd say, in summation, that authority is the antithesis of connectivity, as demonstrated in Network Theory. This is something un-Lacanian that we're introducing into the mix.

ESTHER: Oh, yeah?

YEHUDA: Network Theory is a relatively new paradigm, a cross-discipline thought model: philosophy, physics, sociology. According to this theory, every point in the network is as powerful as the number of its connections. The more connected I am, the more powerful I am. For example, the more information sources I'm connected to, the more information I have. According to the authority approach, you are only connected to your direct superior information sources. But Network Theory argues that there are infinite connections you can benefit from. That's why, in a sense, orphanhood is the opposite of loneliness. By agreeing to be an orphan, one can become less lonely. By letting go of the idea of a single information source, directly superior to you, you can connect to many information sources in all directions. You can switch from authoritarian connectivity to decentralized connectivity, as long as you accept responsibility for your choice.

ESTHER: Yes, decentralized, elastic, fertile, creative connectivity. So, good, we came up with something. I think this part is finished; you know? You see it.

Chapter 2

The Simple Pleasure of the Body

Life begins in the body. The living body is a sensing body and it feels pleasure and pain. It contains orifices through which we relate to our environment. These relationships can be satisfying or frustrating, and the pleasures of the body often inspire shame. "I like my poop," says a child. "Why would you take it away from me?" When children are potty-trained, the relationship between them and the pleasure they derive from their bodies becomes complicated. The child is happy to receive his parents' acknowledgement for defecating in the potty rather than in a diaper or on the floor, but this happiness cannot compete with the happiness of the body.

ESTHER: The word you have chosen to open our second conversation with is pleasure.

YEHUDA: Yes. First, let's admit that we are animals.

ESTHER: First and foremost?

YEHUDA: Absolutely. First and foremost, bodies. We have innated and acquired physiological programming that determines what brings us pleasure. These are mostly erogenous zones, where nerve endings are clustered, making them more sensitive to touch. The sensitivity in these areas is designed according to an evolutionary logic of rewarding certain behaviors such as eating, procreating, and evacuating waste. That's the organic infrastructure. Relationships develop against the backdrop of the organic infrastructure of pleasure, and these relationships can be pro-pleasure or anti-pleasure. As language enters our lives, we can even take pleasure in resisting pleasure.

ESTHER: Meaning, your starting point as a Lacanian is Freud's Pleasure Principle.

YEHUDA: That's right.

ESTHER: Without any deviation?

YEHUDA: No, there is no deviation. I uphold Freud's pleasure principle, as well as what he says in his essay "Beyond the Pleasure Principle."

ESTHER: Okay, so from pleasure we must move further beyond pleasure, both in today's conversation, which starts with pleasure, and in life in general, which begins with a search for pleasure but ends somewhere very different.

DOI: 10.4324/9781003342458-2

YEHUDA: If we want to translate this idea into life ethics, it means honoring pleasure. If I want two and a half sugars in my coffee, I won't ask for one and a half just because two and a half might sound like too much to somebody else.

ESTHER: But you'd gain weight.

YEHUDA: This pleasure comes at the expense of another, that much is true.

ESTHER: Okay, so according to this line of thinking, the question is, which pleasure comes at the expense of another.

YEHUDA: But before it becomes a question of price, it's a question of legitimacy.

ESTHER: Legitimacy that individuals grant themselves?

YEHUDA: Yes, because we start with the question of how we ought to live. And in addressing this question, here's one possible answer: We ought to live our lives without needing other people's approval of our source of pleasure. This is true for adults, not children. But even children ought not to be made ashamed of their pleasure, even if it needs to be limited.

ESTHER: What happens if we shame them?

YEHUDA: Then we're only amplifying the pleasure, turning it into a double pleasure: the pleasure of the action itself, and the pleasure of freedom.

ESTHER: Meaning, they'll want to continue certain behaviors both because they are pleasurable and because they are forbidden.

YEHUDA: Yes. The more we forbid the pleasure by making him feel guilt and shame, the more we define children as free if they enjoy. In this way, we create a logic through which a child would define themselves as free by using their pleasure, thus creating a double pleasure: both for the chocolate and for –

ESTHER: Breaking the rules.

YEHUDA: And the freedom this offence symbolizes.

ESTHER: Would it be accurate to say there are other responses, other structural possibilities of reactions when something is forbidden, and shame is utilized?

YEHUDA: There is the possibility of depression. Giving up pleasure can lead to depression. A lack of pleasure in life will almost surely lead to depression. Ask a depressed person: How are you? Do you enjoy anything? They'll likely say: I don't enjoy anything. Maybe it's because they've given up on pleasure, or maybe it's because they were shamed for their pleasure.

ESTHER: Okay, so you talk about depression as a result of oppression.

YEHUDA: Of course.

ESTHER: You treat the words as etymologically related.

YEHUDA: That's one aspect of depression, though not the only one. In the context of pleasure, a loss of pleasure can lead to depression. Every recovering addict knows this.

ESTHER: So you're saying people ought to develop a friendly relationship with their pleasure. Meaning, they ought to have a respectful dialog with their need for pleasure.

YEHUDA: Yes.

ESTHER: First of all, they should not panic about it. I say this because lots of people have trouble recognizing, defining, and acknowledging their pleasure. We often hear people say "I don't know what I want."

YEHUDA: Especially when it comes to something so basic as the body itself. People might think their pleasure stems from superficial motives and feel apologetic about it. They might ask themselves why they don't crave more meaningful, intellectual pleasure. I had a patient who had trouble acknowledging that she didn't want to date men because she was worried she wasn't pretty enough. It took her a long time to realize it wasn't anything more complicated. It was a basic fear around her body and need for pleasure, the need to feel pretty.

ESTHER: So she gave her inhibition a more sophisticated name and reason than the simple desire to look pretty.

YEHUDA: Right.

ESTHER: And you're saying that we ought to go lower, into the body, so that someone like your patient can say, "The thing that's bothering me is that I don't feel comfortable with my body."

YEHUDA: Correct.

ESTHER: Okay, so is it a cultural thing, this tendency of ours to come up with sophisticated explanations rather than be in touch with our needs?

YEHUDA: It's a historic-cultural tendency, and I dare to say it's a product of Judeo-Christian culture.

ESTHER: Monotheistic culture.

YEHUDA: A monotheistic culture of abstinence and separating body from soul. But I think there's a deeper issue, and I think it comes from the fact that we talk. As Lacan said, "The word has replaced the thing."

ESTHER: That's a central concept of Lacanian theory. What does it mean?

YEHUDA: Instead of a child receiving touch, a breast – something tangible – they receive speech early on and learn to make do with it. Someone says, "That's a good boy," and they take pleasure in that. But it isn't exactly the same as the tangible thing they received earlier in life. There's a shift from the thing to the word, and something gets lost in translation. We've been trained to ignore this loss and make do with words as a substitute. We're used to enjoying praise. I read an article in the newspaper about a kid who found an ancient statuette and received a certificate from the Antiquities Authority. He was taught to make do with a certificate of merit as a substitute for something tangible, like a statuette, which is itself also a substitute image for whatever it represents. As for the patient I mentioned, being pretty isn't the original tangible thing. There are simpler corporeal examples. So I say, we ought to honor the dissatisfaction hiding behind this. We ought to honor the physical, immediate, bodily pleasure, and not belittle its absence. Not be ashamed of missing it, yearning for it, even if we are prepared to give it up, prepared to experience an absence, prepared to skip the sugary treat for the sake of our health. Overweight people were asked for their opinion on appetite reduction medication.

One of them said, "I'm willing to give up food, but not appetite." One way to interpret this statement is that the person will not give up the legitimacy of craving pleasure, even if they're willing to give up the pleasure itself.

We must not make light of the intensity of giving something up. Sometimes we need to mourn this loss because if we don't acknowledge the price, we won't be able to pay it. If I say, "What's the big deal about chocolate? Why am I craving it so much? I'm just being ridiculous," chances are that, ridiculous or not, I'll be binging later that night. Because I haven't given up on it, haven't fostered the proper respect for the chocolate or for foregoing it. If I mourn it properly, I might be able to give it up.

ESTHER: So you're saying, if someone goes on a diet, they ought to go through a period of mourning.

YEHUDA: Yes. Acknowledge the price you're paying. The full meaning of giving something up.

ESTHER: Dieting is very sad.

YEHUDA: Very, very sad. I understand the high price of not eating the chocolate. Or, to be more accurate, of being able to eat the chocolate yet choosing not to. Of giving it up and missing it. I empathize with that pain. Without proper grief and compassion, one cannot say goodbye.

ESTHER: That's a very hedonistic theory.

YEHUDA: You don't need a theory in order to be a hedonist. You need a theory in order *not* to be a hedonist. Let's put it a different way: hedonism is the ideology of perpetuating pleasure. I'm not trying to offer this kind of ideology. I'm offering an attitude of acknowledging and honoring pleasure, whether it is indulged or rejected.

ESTHER: Acknowledging the search for pleasure requires a theory. According to you, we deny the search for pleasure because of our shame, being the owners of this body and its needs.

YEHUDA: Correct.

ESTHER: Because of the word, which made the body too simple, too despicable.

YEHUDA: Right.

ESTHER: The theory you're presenting relies entirely on the basic assumption of pleasure: Acknowledge the pleasure, acknowledge its absence. So we are, on the one hand, and first of all, bodies with drives and needs, and on the other hand, later on, we become talking creatures who use words as substitutes for tangible, bodily sensations. Using a word as a substitute for the thing itself creates a lack. That's the content behind the statement "The word has replaced the thing." Let's clarify that a little more.

YEHUDA: That's a schematic explanation that's easier to understand. A priori, we are body-language creatures. Now let's return to the schematic presentation and I'll give you an example: Two hunters go off to hunt deer in the days of yore. One of them spots the deer, the other does not. So the first wants to tell the second, "There's a deer over there." In this case, the deer is gone. If the deer were there, there would be no need to use the word. Using the word "deer" or even a form of pantomime requires the absence of the deer. Representation appears in the absence of the represented.

ESTHER: So we need words to represent objects in their absence.

YEHUDA: Yes. There's a joke about a three-year-old who never spoke a single word, until one day he suddenly said, "Pass the salt please." His astonished mother said, "Sweetheart, how come you haven't spoken until now?" The kid said, "The salt wasn't missing."

ESTHER: This is what enables mental development: the ability to speak in a time of absence. I'm putting it this way because this point, of the absence of the tangible object, and what takes place in the mind in the time of absence (for instance, the predicament of a child whose mother isn't around to nurse them) is critical for mental development. This is the case according to Klein and Bion, who point to a child's ability to bear this situation as a critical developmental task.

YEHUDA: Pulling this off – which isn't always possible – is a developmental achievement for most people. Replacing the thing itself with a concept; conceptualizing the world. Converting the thing into a word is conceptualizing. As soon as you replace the thing with a word, you can then replace the word with a different word. As soon as organic satisfaction can be replaced with Mommy's kind words, and Mommy's kind words can be replaced with Daddy's kind words, then one can also form bonds with friends. If that's what you mean by "development," that's certainly the case.

ESTHER: The ability to use substitutes.

YEHUDA: Precisely.

ESTHER: So that's a task. Klein defines it as a clear-cut developmental task for a child, being able to use substitutes, to shift from mother to father, from father to siblings, from siblings to teachers and school friends. But look, without noticing, we started with the body and have moved on to the mind. The word has replaced the thing. You say everything starts with the body. Indeed, everything starts with the body, but it certainly can't stay in the body. According to Freud, and Bion after him, where there is contentment there is no mental development.

YEHUDA: Let's go back for a moment to our discussion of the erogenous zones. The anus and the mouth are two orifices through which children experience pleasure for evolutionary reasons. It is through these orifices that they form connections with others, receive sustenance, and metabolize with the outside world. They use them for control. Control and restraint begin with the anus. That is where humans must give up some pleasure and show restraint using their own choice.

ESTHER: This is also reminiscent of Freud. Why do we need restraint? In order to form a civilization? Why give up the pleasure of anal relief? Or, to use simpler, more corporeal language, as would be appropriate for our body-centric discussion: we must give up the pleasure of defecating freely in order to be together, because poop stinks. If everyone pooped constantly, we wouldn't be able to sit together.

YEHUDA: Let's start with the mouth. The mouth is the way we call to another. Children call out to their mothers in order to nurse.

ESTHER: They call their mothers through their mouths and receive sustenance from them through their mouths.

YEHUDA: Right, but it isn't just about food, it's about calling. They call their mothers, they speak. They express their needs and desires through their mouths.

ESTHER: Correct.

YEHUDA: That's how they refer to others.

ESTHER: Meaning, use of the mouth is both symbolic (calling for Mommy) and tangible (actual milk that arrives when the mouth meets the nipple).

YEHUDA: Indeed.

ESTHER: Okay. But what happens with the butt is different.

YEHUDA: The butt is the initial place where children are demanded, where they are required to do the right thing in the right place. They are required to restrain themselves, to give up instant satisfaction, and to delay gratification. The switch from the thing to the word is already a kind of delayed gratification, which manifests in the body through restraint. Once we learn to enjoy the word as a substitute for the thing, a compliment will constitute a substitute for a nipple, and restraint itself constitutes a substitute for release, the pleasure of release. We learn to enjoy restraint as a substitute for the pleasure of release.

ESTHER: Okay. So this is the singularity of the butt: it is the initial place where restraint gets its expression as a central motif in human relationships, where satisfaction is brought on by restraint.

YEHUDA: Restraint that begins in the anal phase migrates later in life into the restraint of holding one's breath while swimming; and a lack of restraint translates as an adult into difficulty in delaying sexual release, causing, in men, premature ejaculation. The people around us can support or negate our pleasure, be it oral – whether the people around a child want them to feel full and have available sustenance – or anal. Anal satisfaction is more complicated, because the parents' job is to negate this pleasure and teach the child to hold it in.

One of the differences between oral and anal pleasure is that children are passive when it comes to oral pleasure. They aren't required to take a stand. When they are hungry they cry, but do not need to make a choice. But in the anal phase children must make a choice: are they prepared to give up the pleasure of instant release in exchange for encouragement from their parents? Now they must become choosers, and enjoy words at the expense of organic pleasure. They begin to enjoy the conceptualization of the thing as a substitute for the thing itself: being told "What a big boy" replaces the pleasure of not holding it in.

This is where things get confusing. The question is whether suffering is found in restraint and pleasure in release, as we tend to believe about animals.

The word complicates things. From the moment it replaces the thing, it becomes an object in its own right, also capable of imparting pleasure. It's a very odd sort of pleasure, different from the one experienced by receiving the thing itself. It is different from the moment when a baby gets exactly what they want into their mouths, then their stomachs.

ESTHER: Because the satisfaction of the word is connected to the absence, the frustration, which is not the case when it comes to milk.

YEHUDA: exactly. That's the satisfaction of frustration, or, better yet, the pleasure of desiring.

ESTHER: In that case, this is the point where pleasure splits from itself and clings to desire, which also contains a pleasurable aspect. So we have the simple pleasure of the body, and then, due to us being lingual creatures, a more complex situation arises: as soon as it replaces the thing, the word receives the status of object, but a lacking one. It contains pleasure, but this pleasure (the pleasure of a compliment, for instance, or of the words of a loved one who is not physically present when they say "I love you") is always a lacking pleasure. Does this not contain satisfaction?

YEHUDA: The experience of satisfaction takes place eventually. The child truly does experience satisfaction at hearing their mother's encouragement, and there is satisfaction in the pleasure of desire as well. One might say, "I feel satisfied by getting my appetite back." It isn't a lack of satisfaction. On the contrary. Surprisingly, words succeed in impersonating things, so the experience of satisfaction does indeed occur.

Chapter 3

On Pleasure and Restraint

The pleasure associated with the mouth (oral), the pleasure associated with the anus (anal), sexual pleasure, and against all bodily pleasures – restraint, the origin of the human ability to produce a civilization.

YEHUDA: We've already said that physical pleasure occurs in erogenous zones, meaning zones in which nerve endings cause stimulation to be experienced as pleasure. We also said that two typical erogenous zones are the mouth and the anus, along with genitals, of course. And we've established that both forms of pleasure, oral and anal, are connected from the beginning to others in the external world. Our surroundings can condone or condemn pleasure. When it comes to oral pleasure, the mother either can or cannot be available to feed her child. The situation with anal pleasure is more complicated, because the parents' role is to condemn pleasure so that the child learns how to hold it in. The question is, what happens when the child is shamed or accused of indulging in their pleasure? What happens to the pleasure then? The pleasure might increase, because forbidding it defines it as a liberty. As soon as a prohibition exists, the child who breaks it has twice as much enjoyment: from eating the cake as well as from defining him or herself as being set free through the act of eating. Forbidding pleasure deems it a symbol of freedom.

ESTHER: Let's linger again on the differences between oral and anal pleasure. If I understand correctly, the main difference is that in the case of anal pleasure, parents are required to condemn it.

YEHUDA: Another difference is that when it comes to oral pleasure, the child is passive and needn't take a stance. But when it comes to anal pleasure, the child must choose: are they willing to give up instant gratification for the sake of verbal encouragement? Now they must become choosing subjects, enjoying words at the expense of organic pleasure. They begin to take pleasure in the conceptualization of the thing rather than the thing itself.

ESTHER: This is analogous to weaning a child from the breast.

YEHUDA: Yes, but there's a difference. Unlike the breast, which is simply taken away, potty training involves a decision the child must make. They must

DOI: 10.4324/9781003342458-3

make a choice to give it up. If a child chooses not to hold it in, and to go in his or her pants, that is a choice.

ESTHER: You've mentioned a connection between potty training and premature ejaculation. Are they associated? The latter is also a matter of choice.

YEHUDA: Premature ejaculation happens when a contradiction occurs between messaging from the anal period, when children learn to be big kids and hold it in, and between the urge for immediate pleasure, which signals to the mind, "Who cares what anyone else thinks? Do what you feel like right here, right now." By showing no restraint and indulging in pleasure without delaying gratification, a man can feel shame, just like the child who loses encouragement when he goes in his pants. That's why it's a recreation of the same kind of situation.

ESTHER: Okay, so let's recap: pleasure and connection to others are both associated with these two orifices – the mouth and the anus. What they have in common is that they are both associated with interpersonal connections on the one hand and with pleasure on the other hand. They are different in the sense that choice only exists in the anal phase. While both involve weaning, oral pleasure is taken away by the mother, leaving the child passive. They can't nurse anymore and don't have a say in the matter.

YEHUDA: The mother can also offer a kind word instead of the breast, which might satisfy the child as a substitute for the pleasure of suckling, but they have no say in the matter. Whether or not they accept the kind words, they must give up the breast. A child weaned off the breast can decide whether to quietly accept the loss, but the loss will happen regardless. On the other hand, a child being potty trained must choose whether or not to give up the pleasure. They can decide to hold on to the pleasure and poop whenever they want to.

ESTHER: But then they'll be losing something else.

YEHUDA: Yes. Then they'd be losing the encouragement.

ESTHER: So the question isn't whether or not to lose something, but rather *which thing* to lose.

YEHUDA: Correct.

ESTHER: Whether to lose the tangible, the Real or the Symbolic.

YEHUDA: True, true.

ESTHER: That is the question.

YEHUDA: That is how parents present it.

ESTHER: That's our life, isn't it?

YEHUDA: It's our life because that's how parents present it. In other words, those are the two options society offers.

ESTHER: I'd say that is the essence of civilization. Am I wrong?

YEHUDA: I agree. The essence of civilization is restraint.

ESTHER: Exactly. Sad, but true.

YEHUDA: It isn't so sad, because when we talk about desire, we talk about the ability to glean the pleasure of satisfaction from restraint.

ESTHER: Oh, dear. Civilization is restraint, but it's other things, too, isn't it? Because otherwise, it sounds too awful. So now let us praise the outcomes of restraint.

YEHUDA: The outcome of restraint is desire.

ESTHER: And desire is the mother of creativity.

YEHUDA: Desire is more or less human life. The human endeavor is to live desirously. That can't happen without restraint to create desire. Anal restraint is only one basic form. The other one that occurs during the same time period is oedipal: one parent is disrupting the child's attempt to live as a couple with the other parent. We usually talk about this in the context of a father who gets in the way of his son's wish to sleep with his mother, which in turn creates desire in the son. The frustration of satisfaction produces desire, and language turns this desire into a kind of satisfaction. That's why someone might say, "I finally got my appetite back." Because appetite, which, ontologically, denotes absence, appears in language as something – a thing that has vanished and happily returned.

ESTHER: This is a key statement. What did you say? Frustration breeds desire, and language turns desire into satisfaction.

YEHUDA: Into pleasure, a kind of pleasure, yes. Which can also be a kind of satisfaction. Desire exists as satisfaction under the condition of language. For instance, there is a kind of aesthetic satisfaction in witnessing minimalist art.

ESTHER: Yes. Are pleasure and satisfaction the same thing in your book?

YEHUDA: Let's define the terms. There are three of them: pleasure, satisfaction, and desire. The pleasure we discussed in the previous chapter is almost entirely made up of satisfaction – answering a physical need. When a physical need is met one experiences relief, a type of pleasure. But there is also pleasure in the title of "big kid," and this pleasure comes from the existence of desire, of giving up satisfaction. It is also a kind of satisfaction.

ESTHER: There are two factors here. One is the symbolic satisfaction of being a big kid, and the other is remaining in desire.

YEHUDA: Yes.

ESTHER: They go together.

YEHUDA: Experiencing desire is actually experiencing pleasure.

ESTHER: Let's linger on this matter of the pleasure of desire. This brings to mind Buddhist thought, which deals with desire no less than Lacan did. It is a central concept in Buddhism. Simplistically speaking, we might say that Buddhist thought is founded on abandoning desire. It's hard to overstate the extremism of this . . . In the Buddha's third truth, he says that in order to stop suffering one must abandon desire. No less than that: abandon it, give it up, turn one's back on it. There are many rich interpretations of this idea, but first and foremost, the message is: let go of desire. Let go of desire because it leads you nowhere but to suffering, and therefore to more desire. And in this sense, if I'm understanding you correctly, you agree with the Buddha.

YEHUDA: I don't think desiring is always suffering. Sometimes it's the opposite.

ESTHER: Desiring isn't suffering?

YEHUDA: In some situations, avoiding desire is suffering. Of course, if suffering stems from frustration, the solution is a lack of desire. But what about the agony of depression? That does not come from frustration. When a person is depressed, they don't say, "I want something and can't have it." They say, "I don't want anything." So for a depressed person, desire and frustration would be solutions. When a depressed patient gets angry that is a sign of healing. Demanding is desiring within a delusion of being owed something, but it's necessary nonetheless.

ESTHER: Hold on. You're saying something radical here, compared to many theologies that directly tie desire to suffering. You're saying they are two separate ideas; that to desire doesn't necessarily mean to suffer.

YEHUDA: Not necessarily. It could be the other way around.

ESTHER: Not desiring is suffering?

YEHUDA: Yes. What does the difference depend on? Anyone who says "desire is suffering" believes that humans are merely animals. Because that would be the case for animals. But as soon as we start talking, things can turn around, because words can change meanings. When I speak, I can refer to something that isn't there. "I have an appetite" means "I have a desire," and so the words turn the lack of food into a thing, a desire. So theologies that refer to desire as innate suffering see humans as living creatures rather than speaking creatures. It's possible that this ethics of identifying desire and suffering sees leaving language as a goal. It's possible that the ideal of the mystical experience is to be beyond language. To be an animal.

ESTHER: That isn't true. Yes, in Buddhism being outside of language is a kind of ideal, and yes, there is a relationship between mysticism and being outside of language, but the goal isn't to return to a pre-verbal state. It isn't animalistic or regressive at all. On the contrary, the goal is to jump ahead to a place beyond pleasure, actually beyond pleasure and pain, desire and suffering altogether. But there is a better way I can put it here: what you give up is your clinging, your attachment to a certain desired object. You can change the object of desire and make it the aspiration for good for all living beings.

YEHUDA: Another thing we can say about desire: why is desire important other than as a source of symbolic pleasure? Desire is essential for the desiring person to exist. Desire is important so that we can have an identity as desirous humans, because humans can be all sorts of things. They can be bodies, egos, what other people think about them. I propose, for the sake of mental well-being, to define ourselves as desiring. Because the alternative is being desired, which is about the ego, about the role we play for others and how we are seen by others and answer their needs. What our function is for others. But if we want to live for our own sake rather than others', we must focus not on how to solve what they lack, but on what *we* lack, on owning this lack and desiring. So why ought we want things? In order to exist. I desire, therefore I am.

Chapter 4

The Ethics of Renunciation

Weaning off the breast breeds a sense of deprivation, which can turn into a permanent stance later in life. It is followed by another withdrawal – potty training. Potty training inspires a sense of prohibition, which can evolve throughout life into a position of insubordination, rebellion, and rage, or, on the contrary, into a blind obedience.

It is possible to grieve change and separation without clinging to it. This becomes possible when one acknowledges that the most important withdrawal humans undergo is of the illusion of deprivation and prohibition.

YEHUDA: Now that we've attained a better understanding of the two withdrawal processes – the oral and the anal – and of the renunciation involved in this withdrawal, let's talk about the ways in which these processes can affect our lives. We'll start with the oral withdrawal – weaning off the breast. At first, the baby – or the adult, if the adult is still a baby – will feel deprived: something deserved was stolen away from them. They still see themselves as the center of the world, for whom everything is intended. If the adult does not move on from this position, they will experience every loss, every defeat, as deprivation, discrimination, a breach of contract –

ESTHER: A kind of broken promise.

YEHUDA: Exactly. As for babies, this is a good outlook for survival, just like a baby bird demanding food from their mother. But what happens when this outlook continues into adulthood? An ethical point of view claims that no one is to blame for this withdrawal. There was never any promise to remain a baby forever, and so nobody is in breach of contract, no one is guilty of depriving you, nor are you guilty for refusing to accept it. There was never any agreement. This realization makes it much easier to accept losses that are nobody's fault. That is the oral aspect. I remember a child who was mad for being deprived by being born his parents' youngest. When I made a big show of siding with him and expressing anger at his parents, he started laughing. He could see the absurdity of his complaint.

DOI: 10.4324/9781003342458-4

The anal loss is a result of a prohibition rather than a deprivation. A child is forbidden from going in their pants. As an adult, one's view can change: a prohibition is imaginary. There is no grownup Other who determines what is and isn't allowed. If I don't feel like going to the bathroom, it's my right to go in my pants. But do I *truly* want that? Perhaps I do, but I'd better not. This is where the human creature is required to make an ethical shift from a rebellious stance to a sober stance, aware of the price of refusal. When it comes to losing the anal object – feces – this loss would mean no longer viewing refusal to go to the bathroom as something one shouldn't do, but as something, they prefer not to do.

ESTHER: Is this the "petit-a" object of Lacanian theory?

YEHUDA: The petit-a object is the missing object, neither the weaned oral nor the forbidden anal.

ESTHER: Neither the breast nor the feces.

YEHUDA: The petit-a object is the one that is lost when language appears.

ESTHER: So that's it! It's an abstraction of both!

YEHUDA: It would be more accurate to say that these objects are the concretization of petit-a, but since they have a place in language, they are not really the undefined "lost thing" that was replaced by the defined, conceptualized object. But yes, it's the principle of what is lost when culture is chosen over pleasure. The cultural core-principle, which appears both in withdrawal from the breast and from the diaper, is speech as a replacement for tangible experience. That is the abstract principle. The petit-a object is the thing that allegedly used to be and disappeared, disappeared because it was replaced by its name. Why do I say "allegedly?" Because anything we can think of – an image, a name – is in itself the outcome of representation – meaning, of language. It isn't truly the thing that used to be there. The ethical stance regarding loss is that it ought to pass through language. That way, rather than the loss leading to an experience of oral deprivation or anal prohibition, it would become the human existential situation. Being a speaking creature, I am sentenced to lose objects, and it is thanks to this loss that I enter language and use it as means of communicating with others.

ESTHER: Would it be appropriate to say, "I must lose tangible objects in order to live in language, in culture?" Does this phrase sound right to you?

YEHUDA: Yes. Thanks to language, something I can't even refer to as "object" is lost. I could call it a "petit-a object," but not an "object" in the way other schools of thought refer to objects such as the oral and the anal. It's hypothetical, something that never truly was, and has only been registered in our consciousness as "lost" following the creation of language. The object (not the petit-a) is a result of language; a verbal or sensual representation.

ESTHER: Okay, so let me rephrase this: the human creature feels that "once upon a time, many, many years ago," there was "something" and this "something" is now lost. But in order to say this, one requires language. And the feeling itself is a result of using language. In this sense, this feeling is an illusion. And this is distinct from the two other losses dealt with in this chapter and the previous one: tangible losses that are a result of the two withdrawals – the oral (weaning off the breast) and anal (potty training).

YEHUDA: Every loss echoes the original loss: of the thing language had banished. Lacanian psychoanalysis can explain an ethics that Buddhism refers to as well – an ethics that instructs us to know how to let go, how to renounce. How to say goodbye. This is relevant to one's deathbed: to know how to leave this world, how to say goodbye to our loved ones. This is the stance faced by the oral and anal choices: we can cling to them as we had to the breast, and thus feel that death is punishment, just as we'd perceived authority during the anal phase.

ESTHER: Now I'd like to share a story from the clinic that can help us clarify the discussion, because in truth the subject we've arrived at is the ethics of dependence, or, in other words, how in the hell can we love anyone or anything, knowing we are bound to lose them? That is one of the greatest questions of existence, and Buddhism has a very interesting answer, as you can see. One woman was in psychoanalysis and had trouble with her clinician. She felt the treatment wasn't helping her and wanted to leave. The longer it went on for, the more anxiety attacks she had. Ultimately, she told her analyst, "This is bad for me, I have to leave." He didn't want to let her go, but she left anyway. Anyone who's been in this situation knows it's an incredibly difficult feat, leaving treatment without the clinician's "permission." It's almost like marrying someone without one's parents' approval.

She started getting medication for anxiety while also advancing in her job, taking several steps she never dared to in the past. Then she came to me for treatment, because she couldn't get over her anxiety. After a brief honeymoon phase, the same symptom recurred while she was with me. I took a month-long leave, which I'd informed her about the first time she got in touch, and shortly after returning from leave I got sick and had to miss sessions again. She complained that it was hard for her when I wasn't available. Then she managed to tell me – I think it was a real accomplishment for her to tell me this – "If I don't like your absences, I'm going to stop seeing you." So I told her, "That's great! I want to treat you, I'd be very glad to continue treating you (that's something I learned from your book[1] "Lacan believed that the psychoanalyst's desire plays a crucial role in how the treatment proceeds. If constitutes reality, then the psychoanalytic reality is constituted by the psychoanalysis's desire" – "I'll be glad to" as a representation of the analyst's desire), but if you want to leave, go ahead and leave." That's what I told her. She was startled to hear that. Now let's return to our discussion of the ethics of dependence. She was shocked to hear that if she didn't want to stay, she could leave, meaning that I did not take on the role of the person who would forbid her from leaving, who could control her choice. What do you think of my response to her?

YEHUDA: Sounds absolutely fine.

ESTHER: I tried to be precise: to tell her she was very welcome here while directing her to acknowledge her freedom. I directed her to acknowledge her freedom, that's what I was offering her. And she panicked because as far as she was concerned, as she told me, if wasn't trying to keep her around, it was a sign I didn't love her.

YEHUDA: As a first step, we can look at what happened to her with her previous clinician, who wouldn't let her go until she finally got away from him.

ESTHER: Right.

YEHUDA: But the moment her second clinician – you – let her go, she felt abandoned.

ESTHER: Exactly.

YEHUDA: Meaning, she needed to envision herself as "unfree" in the first place in order not to feel abandoned, because she pushed her first clinician into the role of warden, which is exactly the anal story. She herself played the anal object that was subjected to the refusal of release, while the clinician was cast in the role of the body. The anal story is about living under prohibition.

ESTHER: So she created the prohibition by casting her clinician in the role of warden so she could then escape him?

YEHUDA: She is like a girl instructed to sit on the toilet without moving until she poops. Supposedly, she'd been controlled and oppressed and was finally able to escape, but when it turned out the alternative was freedom, she wanted to get back into her jail cell. So then when she was with you, she insisted to be obligated, because prison assured her she wouldn't have to deal with real loss. She could camouflage real loss with the prohibition, the deprivation, as if removing them would make everything possible.

ESTHER: And what is that "real loss?"

YEHUDA: The real loss is the fact that even without prohibition or deprivation, every choice has a price, and everything comes to an end. Not because of deprivation or prohibition. The thought that deprivation or prohibition is the cause allows us to believe that if we'd only had better parents, we would be exempt of paying the price of our choices.

ESTHER: The loss of the illusion that I am a beloved being forever, unconditionally.

YEHUDA: Yes.

ESTHER: But that's the constant fantasy. This fantasy is why people get divorced.

YEHUDA: Right. The symptom is the reason for the fantasy not coming true – because the psychoanalyst won't let me leave, because I've been deprived, cheated, short-changed, and if only I'd been treated differently, I wouldn't be lacking. The complaints are, in fact, the symptom, and the symptom is what allows us to pretend that if only we had no reason to complain, there would be no lack. The thing she gave up and fled from under the guise of being forbidden to quit treatment is freedom of choice.

ESTHER: Right.

YEHUDA: Then you gave her freedom of choice, and she panicked.

ESTHER: Yes, exactly. These were panic attacks.

YEHUDA: And panic at freedom of choice is caused by the price – because freedom is the freedom to pay a price. There is no freedom besides the freedom to pay.

ESTHER: There is no freedom besides the freedom to choose the price you are willing to pay . . .

YEHUDA: Freedom is the freedom to choose whether to pay one price or another. And your patient was running away from the payment built into freedom. That's what she was running away from. Rather than admit that she had to give something up, she claimed something was being taken away from her.

ESTHER: To circle back to our starting point, you were saying it was nice to go through life thinking you've been cheated, right?

YEHUDA: Yes.

ESTHER: You were saying that this was one possible outcome of weaning off the breast. A person could go through life preoccupied by what's been taken away from them.

YEHUDA: Yes.

ESTHER: The other outcome is the outcome of potty training – going through life thinking that someone forbade you from doing something; unjustly limited your freedom.

YEHUDA: Correct.

ESTHER: Those are two human choices, thinking "Someone took it from me" or "Someone forbade me." They are choices that define us as the owners of some unfulfilled potential, because people never understood us, because they cheated us.

YEHUDA: Because someone else is to blame for our imperfection. Because potentially, if that someone had done the right thing, we could have been whole.

ESTHER: And so, what you're saying to people is, open your eyes, see that you are un-whole, and see that the reason you are un-whole isn't your mother, who weaned you out of lack of generosity. She had to wean you anyway.; and see that you can't poop your pants and continue to live in a society, because the two just don't go together.

YEHUDA: To be part of civilization, of the human club, you can't poop your pants. Why? Because the club won't accept you, not because it's wrong or forbidden, but because that's how things work.

ESTHER: The rule at this club is that people who poop their pants aren't allowed.

YEHUDA: That's the rule.

ESTHER: For becoming a member of the club.

YEHUDA: Exactly. Or you can decide not to give up that right. You're free to choose.

ESTHER: So, you're confronting people with the fact that they made a choice, that they are making a choice.

YEHUDA: Yes, that they made a choice and are still making one now.

ESTHER: What used to be enforced is now a choice.

YEHUDA: No! It was a choice from the very beginning! The historical loss is also something they chose to do.

ESTHER: Why do you say that? Do children choose to be potty trained?

YEHUDA: Children choose to be potty trained in the sense that when their parents tell them, "No pooping in your pants," they say, "All right, I'll obey." What they are really saying is, "I choose to pay this price." They choose to be obedient, to avoid the other price. So, the goal is ultimately for people to see themselves as making a choice, even in retrospect. To help them see they are telling themselves a story about deprivation and a story about prohibition when they could have been viewing at least some of their misfortunes as choices. Here's a wonderful statement: It's never too late to have a happy childhood. Meaning, one can, in retrospect, position oneself at a different point of view regarding the events of one's childhood and acknowledge that they were, to a certain extent, a choice, or, to a certain extent, a helpless circumstance. Either way, no one is to blame. Sure, some state laws would determine that the parents are to blame, but the adult child ought not to point fingers, because then they would be escaping their responsibility to face the structural lack. Nevertheless, the child can still choose to accuse according to their chosen ethics, and there are certain treatment scenarios where laying blame is recommended.

ESTHER: In other words, if we're dealing with ethics, when it comes to these two unhappy childhood moments, the two withdrawals, you believe in the principle of absolute choice. Pure choice.

YEHUDA: There are plenty of things we don't choose.

ESTHER: But you face them with an act of choice.

YEHUDA: We ought to define the line between choices and non-choices from the start. Even *that* is a choice – deciding what is a choice and what isn't . . . Some people elect a worldview according to which they had chosen to be born to their parents. Believing this is a choice. I accept that – not the specific choice, but the fact that it *is* a choice, because we determine the limits of our choices. Let's start from the end: I choose everything, and that's a difficult concept to accept. Since it's difficult, I choose to put caveats on that statement. And then, to lighten my load, I choose what to define as non-choice territory. I can play around with that territory.

ESTHER: But, yes, I choose everything. For starters, I choose everything. It's an absolute statement: I choose everything. And now let's play around with it because it's unbearable.

YEHUDA: And then you can ask yourself: your attitude at age four – can you acknowledge that was a choice? Maybe not at age three, but at age four, yes, that's where I draw the line. Why there? Because. No one can tell me where to draw the line. There is no big Other to tell me where to draw the line between choice and constraint.

ESTHER: And that is the loneliness from which choice is derived: there is no big Other to choose for me.

YEHUDA: That's why no one can question my pleasure, either. Why do I like my coffee with one sugar? Any answer to that question would have to depend on some master who instructed me to choose this way. So I don't even want to answer that question. I just want sugar in my coffee.

ESTHER: So there is nothing beyond choice. To me, that is the great loss. To go back to that patient who needed her clinician to refuse to let her go –

YEHUDA: Indeed, she was right. She was right to feel abandoned, but she misunderstood how exactly she was being abandoned. She thought she was abandoned by a mother who didn't love her enough.

ESTHER: When in fact, she was abandoned by that big Other who suddenly ceased to exist . . .

Note

1 Israely, Y. (2018) *Lacanian Treatment Psychoanalysis for Clinicians*. New York: Routledge.

Reference

Israely, Y. (2018) *Lacanian Treatment Psychoanalysis for Clinicians*. New York: Routledge.

Chapter 5

The Subject, the Other, and the Object Between Them

This chapter will tackle our difficulty in acknowledging and owning our drives due to our shame for having drives in the first place. It will discuss the way we turn the Other into someone who makes demands (on our love, our devotion, our wisdom, and our money); the way in which, when the Other does demand something from us, we renounce our ownership of desire ("I did it because the kids asked me to," "I have to work overtime because my partner loves money"); and our refusal to "do what we're asked to do" – meaning, what we want to do . . .

ESTHER: There's this writer who I think is brilliant, but she won't show her talents. She's never published anything, though she's written several books. That's the real reason she came to treatment. Recently I've been encouraging her to make her art public. This is a decision I've made, even though I know I'm supposedly putting my desire ahead of hers. But I don't think that's truly the case. I think I'm representing her desiring voice. I told her, "You want to publish. You're yearning to publish."

She said, "I'm still not convinced there's a good *reason* to publish."

I said, "That's interesting. Whose job is it to convince you? Why is it even about convincing? What is the purpose of that word here, in this room, between us?" I said, "It's simple. Writing is your thing. You live; therefore, you have no choice but to write and be a writer in the world."

She asked, "But what significance does my art have? What does it contribute?"

"In principle, it contributes nothing," I said. "You hear the bird chirping outside? That's all it is. Your art is your chirping, and it's a shame to keep it locked up inside, that's all."

YEHUDA: The two withdrawals we discussed in the previous chapter require renunciation. Renunciation means acknowledging that nobody owed me the thing that was given to me or deprived of me, the thing that was taken away, in the oral or anal phase (respectively). When one acknowledges this, they realize there is no one to "convince" them to produce anything. It's entirely up to them to produce if they want to, or not. In the story of the binding of Isaac, God demands Isaac

DOI: 10.4324/9781003342458-5

from Abraham. One version[1] of this story contains a variation: after God orders Abraham to leave the child alone and offers a stag to take Isaac's place at the altar, Abraham still wishes to draw a bit of Isaac's blood. Meaning, Abraham asks God to make his demand so it can continue to serve as a reason for the subject's action. It's hard to give up the Other's demand, hard to give up the Other, hard to agree to be orphaned. That's why this writer who needs to be convinced structures her own desire as the demand of another. Just like the patient who wanted a clinician to demand that she stay in treatment, this writer is positioning you as the one forcing her to go public, desiring her desires for her.

ESTHER: Meaning, in the case of the patient we discussed in the previous chapter, she turned me into the one who wanted her to be in treatment, and thus she is forced to stay rather than choosing to stay.

YEHUDA: Right. This structure of being "demanded" exists in order to fulfil my wishes without admitting to them. Like the writer, who needs somebody to require that she publish in order to make her own wishes come true – in order to express herself.

ESTHER: She asks to be convinced, meaning, she hides her own desire behind another's.

YEHUDA: Exactly. "Come force me to do what I want." But it's tragic, tragic, because at the next level, if anyone takes the bait and tries to convince her, she'll rebel. "No way! I won't do what you tell me! I'm a free person!" It's a paralyzing freedom.

ESTHER: "Come make a demand that I can refuse."

YEHUDA: No, "Come make a demand that I express myself, and now that I've deluded myself that you're the one making the demand rather than me making a wish, let me rebel and reject the demand."

ESTHER: Right, but why not acknowledge the desire in the first place?

YEHUDA: Being ashamed of one's drives. Let's say, for instance, that I'm a performer who's ashamed of his exhibitionistic drive, and I'll only be persuaded to perform if the audience absolutely can't live without me. That way, I don't have to acknowledge the drive behind my actions, but rather pretend to be pushed into action by another's demands.

ESTHER: You mean the reason we hide behind another's wishes is our own shame?

YEHUDA: Shame for having desires in the first place.

ESTHER: Why? Because of the nature of the desire, which is somehow foolish or embarrassing?

YEHUDA: Because we are civilized creatures. We've been brought up not to spread our feces around, not to demand our desires from others (during the oral phase), and not to stand out in our exhibitionism. That's what civilization trained us to do – repress our drives. Because these drives are suppressed by the Other, we've come up with a ruse: We recruit the Other to demand that we act on our drives.

ESTHER: But then we're trapped, right? We're trapped because we tell ourselves it isn't our desire, but the desire of the Other, and if we're obsessive – meaning, if we believe there's reason to be angry – we think, "Oh, so you want me to do that? In that case, I won't do it."

YEHUDA: Correct.

ESTHER: In cases of obsessiveness.

YEHUDA: Yes, that's how it goes if the demand takes the form of a threat on individuality. As in: doing something for another means I'm not free, so I'll refuse to do the thing I wanted to do in the first place. The detour through the wishes of another causes me to go into reverse.

ESTHER: To return to the binding of Isaac, Abraham's insistence on drawing blood, practically begging for it, is traditionally interpreted as heroism, as devoutness. It goes to show you how devout Abraham is, and how merciful God is. Let's interpret the Other's behavior here: Why does God ultimately reject the binding of Isaac? He leaves Abraham wanting, leaves him with nothing but symbolism. The stag is merely a replacement for his first-born.

YEHUDA: Let's treat this entire story as Abraham's fantasy. Abraham needs to believe in a figure that makes demands on him, and he creates one for this purpose. The demanding figure? I'd rather treat Abraham as the demander. What does Abraham demand? That is the question. He demands to be demanded, as a sign of the existence of the Other. "I am demanded therefore there is a demander." While in fact, the Other does not exist. That's my point.

ESTHER: How so?

YEHUDA: There's nobody to convince us to step out into the light. It's like you told your patient – you're a bird, you're going to chirp anyway, and so one can assume you'd like to chirp out in the world. Am I wrong? Would you rather chirp only at home? Then go ahead and be silent for the rest of your life. The patient wants you to convince her. But why should you convince her? *She* should convince *you* that it's better to be silent. She needs to acknowledge that she comes to treatment so that you can convince her to publish. The timing of this interpretation must be prudent. You have to be careful not to provoke the patient so much that she quits treatment just to prove you wrong.

ESTHER: Yes. The great Other does not exist, as you said. But how so? Putting most of the weight on the drive and less on the object of the drive is an adherence to Freudian thought. A major criticism of Freud's successors was that they deemed the object of the drive – the mother or the father, whatever object the drive gloms onto – marginal compared to the drive itself. Freud seemed to say that the drive would find objects to attach to. In that sense, he claimed the same as you: the Other is less critical.

YEHUDA: Not in that sense, no. I think the Other *is* critical. It is critical in forming desire.

ESTHER: An Other is necessary in forming desire. Why is that?

YEHUDA: The Oedipal father needs to set a limit on the child's pleasure in order to create desire.

ESTHER: The Other is there to provide a prohibition for the purpose of withdrawal.

YEHUDA: For the purpose of withdrawal, and therefore for the purpose of desire. For instance, some people interpret attention disorders as *jouissance*, as a lack of boundaries. Even from a neurological point of view, the inhibition function in the prefrontal cortex is missing. By setting boundaries, parents allow delay, concentration, the ability not to jump from one stimulus to the next. In this sense, castration serves as an enabler.

ESTHER: But there is no castration in the case of attention disorder.

YEHUDA: Precisely. According to the Freudian concept of castration, a father forbids the child's jouissance. In Lacanian thought, castration creates desire, creates attention.

ESTHER: So this is Lacan's addition: the castration – the limitation – creates desire.

YEHUDA: Yes. The Oedipal story is a myth regarding the function of language in human life, a castration that creates desire. In this sense, the Other is critical, not only in that it opposes instinct, but in that it supports desire. Lacan, who interpreted Freud in this way, discussed Strachey's translation of the word "*trieb.*" According to Lacan, Strachey made a mistake when he translated "*trieb*" as "instinct," because the correct translation would be "drive." Instinct is an organic need that animals have as well, whereas drive is a need that was transformed by interaction in language with others. Something that contains symbolic elements, something between the Real and the Symbolic. What creates drive is not only biology, but also the restriction of pleasure. Supposedly by the figure of the father, and that's where the fantasy of the demander comes from, but in fact the limit is set by the structure of language itself. By the fact that language, being a mediator, is already a step removed from the hypothetical, full, unmediated pleasure.

ESTHER: Freud says that drive is located on the border between body and mind. You're saying it's on the border between Real and Symbolic. That isn't too far off.

YEHUDA: Right, it's the same idea. And then, when we treat the drive as partially caused by a restriction posed by an Other, Abraham can say all sorts of things about his relationship with God. And if we put aside the fact that we are appalled by the idea of sacrifice – because I'm talking about the desire in this story – Abraham can say, "By taking away the child object, God leaves an absence inside of me, which is a foundation of desire." For instance, chasing the symbolic stature of father of the Jewish nation – that is a symbolic purpose that replaces the concrete child. Abraham can suppress this and say, "I am in awe of God" without realizing that God is functioning as the creator of desire.

ESTHER: I don't understand. I'd like further explanation.

YEHUDA: He can fear God, feel that God is limiting his freedom, and that if it weren't for God, he'd be able to do as he pleases – protect his son. For Abraham, God's function is to demand the object, thus demanding that he enter desire.

In the next phase, Abraham treats God as someone fulfilling a function in his own soul, and so when God quits His position as demander and say, "Forget your child, I'm not interested in him," Abraham argues, "How about just a drop of blood? Can we please continue this dynamic in which you are the big, demanding Other, I am the subject, and Isaac is the object?" When Abraham acknowledges needing the Other's demand, it's like your writer patient becoming aware that she was asking you to demand that she publish so she can fulfil her own desire to do so. This is the triangle: Other, subject, and object. The Other is cast in the role of demanding the object from the subject.

ESTHER: Something (an object) that the Other demands from the subject . . . Meaning, a triangle is created – a forced subject, a demanding Other, and an object –

YEHUDA: An Object between them.

ESTHER: An object between them . . . And you? What do you do? How do you intervene as clinician?

YEHUDA: Are you asking about the purpose of treatment?

ESTHER: Yes.

YEHUDA: The purpose of life. We're discussing life in this book. The purpose of life is for people to own their desires, and the Other's function in these desires is to play roles assigned by the subject in order to create desire through their relationship. We can cast the Other as demander, as customer, as structure positioning us in roles in which we always produce whatever we want to produce.

ESTHER: It's like if a guy says his wife "pushes him to be creative." Take ownership of your own phantasm!

YEHUDA: Exactly. Work with your phantasm while knowing it's a phantasm. Then the obsessive phantasm is, "I must give because someone is demanding." But as long as it is unaware, they end up adding "So I won't give it." But when there's awareness, one can give in to demands while knowing it's just a game, and that in truth we are doing the thing we want to do.

Some people set an alarm in the evening, then break the clock in the morning. "Who is he to tell me when to wake up?!" But they are the ones who set the alarm, and they did it for their own good . . . They choose to deny this. They choose to define the clock as enslaving them. Alternatively, they can be aware that they themselves had set the alarm, and that they are waking up to do the work of their own desire.

Note

1 7. AND THE ANGEL OF THE LORD CALLED UNTO HIM OUT OF HEAVEN, AND SAID: ABRAHAM.
    LAY NOT THY HAND UPON THE LAD, etc. Genesis 21:12. Where was the knife? Tears had fallen from the angels upon it and dissolved it. 'Then I will strangle him' said he [Abraham] to Him. 'LAY NOT THY HAND UPON THE LAD'. was the reply.

'Let us bring forth a drop of blood from him' he pleaded. 'NEITHER DO THOU ANY THING TO HIM' He answered 'inflict no blemish upon him'.

Babilonian Talmud: Midrash Raba to Humash Bereshit, Parashat Yayera 76: on mount Moriya, the binding of Isaac. TRANSLATED INTO ENGLISH WITH NOTES, GLOSSARY AND INDICES UNDER THE EDITORSHIP OF RABBI DR. H. FREEDMAN, B.A., PH.D. AND MAURICE SIMON, M.A. THE SONCINO PRESS LONDON First Edition 1939.

Reference

Babilonian Talmud: Midrash Raba to Humash Bereshit, Parashat Yayera 76: on mount Moriya, the binding of Isaac. TRANSLATED INTO ENGLISH WITH NOTES, GLOSSARY AND INDICES UNDER THE EDITORSHIP OF RABBI DR. H. FREEDMAN, B.A., PH.D. AND MAURICE SIMON, M.A. THE SONCINO PRESS LONDON First Edition 1939.

Chapter 6

Oedipus

This chapter will discuss being an unwanted child;
Being an overly wanted child whose mother won't give him up;
Being rejected and how being rejected can be a pretty good solution;
Being wanted, but not too much, so that one can move on from one's relation-
ship with Mom;

And about the tragic maternal role, which requires a mother to give up her son
so that he might discover his father, and other worlds.

We believe parents will find this chapter particularly useful.

YEHUDA: A child goes through several rungs in the Oedipal ladder. The starting point in this process is the question of whether they were born wanted or unwanted. If they are unwanted, they are completely unnecessary creatures. This might make them want to die, simply because nobody wants them to exist. Anaclitic depression may develop as a result. The outcome can be acute psychosis, existence as an unnecessary object.

Assuming a child is wanted by his mother, the next step can be being wanted too much, in the sense that a mother refuses to release him. That makes him a different kind of object – a precious or significant object, but not free to stop being a branch in a tree or a limb in a body and start being a body in its own right. This is where the experience of paranoia comes up; the experience of constantly being limited by the tree one is a branch of, the tree being a structure they cannot detach from.

The next step, the third in the ladder, is that the condition for detachment is being rejected. And this includes fantasies of rejection. When do people imagine they are rejected? When this offers a solution for the feeling of being stifled by being overly wanted. In this sense, I am rejected, therefore I am, otherwise I'm part of symbiosis. This is the kind of person who gets themselves fired instead of quitting.

ESTHER: What does "the next step" mean?

YEHUDA: A little more separateness. A step beyond being a limb of a body is being a hewn limb.

DOI: 10.4324/9781003342458-6

ESTHER: Hang on. There is the first rejection, the real one, where a baby can be so rejected that they die.

YEHUDA: He isn't "rejected" because he was never "un-rejected." He never belonged. He is unwanted. "Rejected" means you were once wanted and no longer are, you're being pushed away, thrown out.

ESTHER: Okay. So this rejection you discuss as the third step –

YEHUDA: Yes, it's the masochistic position of a person defining themselves as rejected.

ESTHER: You've moved on from psychosis to perversion.

YEHUDA: Correct. The psychotic is a paranoid who cannot detach, and the masochist invents a trick for disconnecting in order to live, a way to chop himself off like a branch cut from a tree, removing himself from the one refusing to let him go by telling himself a story about being rejected. Now the question is how aware he is. If this is a perverted structure, a person engaged in rituals in which he is humiliated, then he is relatively aware. I'm saying he's aware because he takes pleasure in the position of being rejected. While the person with a psychotic structure has no choice but to be positioned as an inseparable limb of a body, the perverse person – and the masochist, as a sub-category of perversion – manages to detach themselves. Unlike the post-oedipal neurotic, in the perverse structure the function of the father who sets limits is missing so there is no way to be loved by the mother as well as separated from her by the father. That's why the masochist needs to be rejected by her in order to set themselves free. When humiliated, they still belong as object, as property. As rejected, they are discarded as object, but there is no other way to be set free. But we can all feel rejected here and there in order to exclude ourselves from feeling too important. That's why often when a patient brings up feelings of rejection, I try to check how they would feel if things went the other way. Or, in the opposite situation, when a person is overburdened and feel like no one can survive without them, I ask if they'd prefer to be rejected. Meaning, the question is where we are positioned in our fantasy, not in reality. Where are we in our fantasy, on the ladder between "necessary" and "rejected."

ESTHER: Therefore, the rungs of the ladder are the phases of the spectrum between "wanted" and "rejected."

YEHUDA: Not exactly. The phases are stations on the way to existing as a subject. The first station is being unnecessary, the next is being symbiotic, and the third, the one we're discussing now, is the masochistic solution for symbiosis: being rejected. There is a gap between the conscious ladder and the unconscious ladder. If I'm consciously complaining about being rejected, then I could be unconsciously indulging in being free. If I'm consciously complaining about how I'm so needed that I don't have a moment to myself, I'm unconsciously indulging in how important I am. Now, a person can truly be rejected, outcast as a child, and afraid of being rejected again. And in this case, I would say, all right, here is the reason for the problem, now let's try and find out why you are holding onto it, why you are sticking to it. What purpose does it serve? It's still relevant to ask how one would feel if they were too important instead. Biography is not an all-encompassing excuse.

ESTHER: Yes, okay, let's stay with this jailbreak, this symbiosis that in order to break free from we must ask someone to abuse us.

YEHUDA: Correct. "Hit me," "Hurt me," "Humiliate me" – those are different ways of requesting rejection.

ESTHER: "Reject me," "ridicule me."

YEHUDA: No, "ridicule me" is not the basic thing. There are all sorts of forms: hit me, ridicule me, humiliate me – they are all saying something more basic: reject me. And the even deeper thing hiding beneath "reject me" is "I'm free."

ESTHER: On the other hand, is the problem actually solved during the masochistic ritual? A person in a masochistic ritual is turning themselves into an object. You describe this as a solution? Yet they still aren't a subject. They're still serving as another's object. So, what have we accomplished?

YEHUDA: They remain an object either way. The question is, are they a consumed object or a rejected object. Being a rejected object is a solution to paranoia. It offers an improved substitute for the other possibility – being someone who cannot break free at all.

So, indeed, they are still not a subject. They are still not an independent body, but rather a limb on another body, but at least they are a removable limb, that doesn't always have to be attached. They can breathe. A paranoid can't breathe, because they are constantly surrounded.

ESTHER: Meaning, the perverted act of demanding rejection allows them to break out of the stifling symbiosis. If they are wanted all the time, they are not free to be themselves, and they feel stifled. That is the paranoid psychosis. Masochistic perversion is agonizing too, but by performing the ritual of rejection, they can release themselves from those pursuing them.

YEHUDA: But there's another twist we oughtn't ignore: in psychosis, just as the paranoid is his mother's object, her nipple is his object. There is a mutual holding on.

ESTHER: You're talking about his mind; his inner world.

YEHUDA: Yes.

ESTHER: In his mind, things are arranged so that he is using and being used.

YEHUDA: The part he is aware of is that he is being used. The less aware part is that he won't let go. There's a fable about capturing a monkey: a hunter places a nut inside a hole in a tree, then waits for the monkey to reach in and grab it. With his fist closed around the nut, the monkey's hand becomes stuck in the hole. Being a monkey, he won't let go of the nut to release his hand. In order to be captured, the condition is that you yourself must hold onto the nut and refuse to let go. The psychotic has an object he won't give up, and that is why he can't set himself free.

ESTHER: How would you call this object? Why do you refer to it as a nipple?

YEHUDA: The nipple is one of the representations of this object. A petit-a object is the abstract name.

ESTHER: Okay, but now you've confused me and probably the readers, too.

YEHUDA: Have I?

ESTHER: Let's look at this through the mother-son model. I'm missing a few information links in order to understand the concept of a "petit-a object." Let's imagine a child whose mother loves him so much she won't let him go anywhere. She needs him at home with her, which drives him crazy. This is something I've seen more than once. Many cases of paranoid schizophrenia look like this – a mother refusing to let her child go. You're saying that not only is the mother holding onto the child, but the child is holding onto the nipple. As far as I'm concerned, in terms of the symbols I'm familiar with from other schools of psychoanalysis, the term "nipple" represents a partial object, a milk supplier. There is no "mother" subject, but a milk supplier, and this is how the relationship is defined. A child needs milk supply. For example: a 30-year-old schizophrenic who won't give up the allowance her 55-year-old mother gives her, even though she has a monthly income.

YEHUDA: Let's put aside the question of the nature of the mother–child relationship, because the quality of the relationship is irrelevant. Let's go back to our discussion before the nipple. The signifier "nipple" might be too confusing because of the meaning it receives in different schools of thought.

The castration – be it succeeding in being a hewn limb or succeeding in being a person who lacks something, which is being a castrated body – the castration is the rift between things themselves and their naming in language. The question is whether or not we use language. The more primordial, un-signified creature, the one who does not use words, does not give up on the thing itself. They won't substitute the thing for its name. They want the thing and will not or cannot make do with the substitute – its name. A dog, for instance, can enjoy a kind word as well as a treat during the training process. A trained dog is part of the human order. But in nature, where human language is meaningless, the only satisfaction comes from food. The way they are built, perhaps as a result of an unmediated relationship with the mother, won't allow them to use the name as a substitute for the thing itself. Had their relationship been mediated, it would have been mediated by language. The psychotic mind often protests the very existence of the myth within which we live. In this sense, psychotics strive for radical truth. They have trouble participating in normative lies. A psychotic would never say that her son is the most handsome boy at school "and I'm not just saying that because I'm his mother." She would say he's below average, maybe even ugly, because it's the truth.

ESTHER: There is no mediation because there's no need for mediation.

YEHUDA: The mother of the schizophrenic woman you described, who never gave her any space, did not need to be named because she never left. That's why language had no function, no mediating role. Language did not replace the missing thing, because the thing was ever-present. When the thing is ever-present, there is no need to point to it. Only in its absence is a word required to represent it. Language is how we think about something in its absence, and that is not required in the case of a mother who is always around. That thing, the pre-lingual object, the thing that does not yet have a name, is the petit-a object. That is the precise definition of the petit-a object.

ESTHER: The thing that has no name.

YEHUDA: The thing we cannot say anything about. Saying "nipple" is saying something, it's naming. We're trying to tell a story about something that used to be, but even calling it "something" is missing the point, because it's already naming it.

ESTHER: Yes. This is an essentially impossible discussion.

YEHUDA: That's why Lacan says we cannot discuss this thing: because it isn't accessible by language. The mere appearance of language depends on the absence of the thing. That's when we can say, "This thing that is inaccessible to language," or, in short, "a." "A chair," "a table." It's the word's label.

ESTHER: Okay, I get it now, it's the article that precedes the noun, and the thing denoted by it.

YEHUDA: Correct. And when it remains on its own, it represents the absence of the noun, the table or the chair. Meaning, the thing that existed before the word is what the psychotic won't let go of.

ESTHER: Right.

YEHUDA: They will not – or cannot – accept this agreement, in which the "thing," the "a," is renounced in exchange for language, a name. They won't give it up, and therefore language becomes less valid for them.

ESTHER: Not "less valid," but valid in a different way.

YEHUDA: Because they would not pay for the validity of language by renouncing the pre-lingual object.

ESTHER: Okay, there's a Bion book called *Transformations*,[1] in which he says a psychotic person uses language in a completely different way, and for completely different needs. For the psychotic, the name is not a substitute for the thing but is "the thing itself." Bion discusses "bizarre objects." They are not representations, not names, but also not tangible objects – they are between the Real and the Symbolic. They are the pursuers the psychotic attempts to flee. You talk about the petit-a object, and Bion talks about "bizarre objects," which are neither language nor creatures given to sense experience, and with which the psychotic has a pursuing dynamic. It's interesting how you often emphasize the matter of choice, but now that we're discussing psychosis you've changed courses, saying it isn't a choice, an active rejection of castration, but rather a lack of need, or, I should say, incapacity, to give up the object for the name.

YEHUDA: It's something on the line between "they were born this way" and "they made an unconscious choice." The question of how responsible we are for our choices or how unconscious our choices are is a whole different subject, and that's why we're still on the line.

ESTHER: But in other cases, you are unequivocal with regards to choice, conscious or unconscious. In truth, the patient's choice is something the treatment points at, steers towards, leading the treatment to acknowledge it and finally actualize it.

YEHUDA: That's true with regards to neurotics. I view neurotics as choosing their position, and the more I treat them as capable of making their own choices, the better the treatment goes. With a psychotic, things can go the other way – attributing a psychotic with unconscious intentions might in itself awaken paranoia.

ESTHER: Can you explain why? Why is it that pointing to a psychotic person's unconscious intention or choice makes them feel pursued?

YEHUDA: Because for the psychotic person, when I talk about an unconscious choice – or the unconscious in general – I'm talking about an Other that seems to exist within them, making choices for them. It's an unconscious object that controls them, determining their fate. This is precisely the paranoid experience. Now they're going to look behind their shoulders constantly, to see if their unconscious is following them. "Determining their fate" – that's paranoia.

ESTHER: Yes. And that's exactly the difference between the neurotic and the psychotic. For the neurotic, the schism between the thing itself and the name that represents it – the name as metaphor that substitutes for the object itself – is part of a more general substitution. There is the substitute of mother for father, of one meaning for another: Metaphor. The neurotic understands metaphor, and so they can assume there are other, unconscious meanings behind the things they say. For the psychotic, insinuating hidden meanings is a threat, because they cannot assume their existence as symbolic beings. Instead, they perceive them as a reality of pursuit.

YEHUDA: I agree. The psychotic is out of the realm of choice so there is no way for them to hold the thought of an unconscious choice. For neurotics, the concept of the "unconscious" is one of the greatest graces Freud imparted to humankind: by conceptualizing the unconscious, he created a distinction between "blame" and "responsibility." Meaning, the unconscious is like a trick that allows us to say that something is a choice, and therefore our responsibility, but not our fault, because this choice took place without our conscious awareness.

ESTHER: Meaning, in the language of the school of object relations, responsibility is the depressive stance, as opposed to haunting guilt, which is the schizo-paranoid stance.

And another thing: Rabbi Kook discusses guilt and blame. He argues that guilt is needless self-involvement that doesn't lead to improvement. If a person feels they have sinned or hurt someone, Rabbi Kook claims they ought to correct their actions in the real world rather than wallow in guilt. This is one of the reasons Yom Kippur, which is devoted to reflection on one's misdeeds, only lasts a single day. The rest of the year we ought to work to change and correct our attitude and – as a result – reality.

Let's return to the initial question: you're discussing castration because the Oedipal phase is the phase of castration, correct?

YEHUDA: Yes. In the castration ladder, we've reached the masochist's rung. Let's remember that masochism is just one example. There is an entire array of perversions that symbolize similar ideas. Fetishists, for instance, identify with objects, behaving like organs that can be disconnected from the body. The role of the father as an alternative to the mother is not fully present in the perverse structure. There is still no alternative to mother – still no father from the original story. I say, "the father from the original story," because in each of our lives, unlike in the original classical story, the father is a function that can be filled by many people and objects. The role is called "father," but can be filled by grandma, or even by someone who only exists in Mother's speech. What counts is hearing Mother say, "I'm not the only one. There are other authorities, other people you can have a relationship with besides me."

ESTHER: So, does that mean the mother we've been discussing until this point is the kind of mother who presents herself as the one and only?

YEHUDA: That's right. It's the kind of mother you're trapped with and can only be released by way of rejection. But if there is another authority, someone who either exists in reality or someone she talks about, pointing to with her speech, they can release you, offering their hand as an alternative to Mother's hand, adding something else that Mother doesn't. Another person. The paternal metaphor.

ESTHER: Talking about another authority, or the actual existence of somebody like that, adds a third party. And in this sense, when there is a third person, there is someone to escape to.

YEHUDA: Yes, there's an alternative. And as a result, it's also how we learn to count to three. Even certain learning disabilities can be the result of a difficulty in moving from two to three. This "third person" is a metaphor, and a metaphor is substituting one thing for another, another thing that adds meaning. As opposed to metonymy, which is a transitional object, an object that is merely a representation of the mother and adds nothing by itself. Now the question is, what is the relationship with the father? We can be angry with him for taking our mother away; we can love him for rescuing us from Mother; we can love him for the person he is; we can enter a love triangle – Father loves Mother and Mother loves me, or I love Mother and Mother loves Father. With regards to a love triangle, I have a recommendation for a direction to take: the child ought to turn their gaze from Mother to Father, meaning out toward the world. A child ought to love their father more than their mother, to be focused on their father and view him as a gateway to the world. When we love our father, we can later love somebody else, a fourth and fifth person. This is how we enter the world. It's a good idea to transfer the libidinal charge outwardly, onwards from Mother.

ESTHER: You don't say! So many mothers of children ages three-four, even younger, complain about how their child loves their father better; how they long for their fathers, charmed by them . . .

YEHUDA: Of course, being a mother is the most thankless job in the world.

ESTHER: A mother, although being abandoned in this sense, can be happy when her child is charmed and enamored with somebody else.

YEHUDA: That's right. The mother should acquiesce to this, even though it hurts. Like any other job, the better one performs it, the more redundant they become, which is painful and positive all at once. That's how a clinician feels at the end of a successful course of treatment, when the patient moves on with their lives.

ESTHER: True. It's so good for us to be saying this. It can offer mothers not only a direction but a comfort.

YEHUDA: Correct.

ESTHER: It's a comfort to know their child is developing well, and that they've done their job well.

YEHUDA: Yes. They have a confident child prepared to step out into the world. Father is the gateway to the world. And Father should love Mother. The best thing a father can do for their child is love the child's mother.

ESTHER: Why is that?

YEHUDA: To teach the child to love someone besides themselves. By loving their child, fathers teach their children to love themselves. By loving their children's mothers, fathers teach their children to love, period. They teach them about loving relationships.

ESTHER: But the father can accomplish this by loving another woman besides his child's mother, right? I'm thinking about divorced parents, or other scenarios where a father-mother love is not possible. If fathers want their children to learn how to love, isn't it enough for them to see love around them? Can their father love a man or a woman rather than their mother?

YEHUDA: The triangle is important.

ESTHER: I understand. But why? Because the child must renounce their mother? Because the father must triumph over them? Is that it? You're hinting at Oedipal defeat. You believe defeat is a vital part of the Oedipal story. Right? Is defeat the castration?

YEHUDA: Yes. Losing the battle against one's father in order to win the war against life. And things do get complex when it comes to, well, complex families.

ESTHER: That's right. Sometimes we can practically see the lack of defeat in the Oedipal phase, the lack of a renunciation of the attempt to be the mother's only object.

YEHUDA: I think the Oedipal complex takes place anyway. It doesn't matter if the parents are married or if Father has a boyfriend. Oedipus is there regardless.

ESTHER: What are you referring to as "Oedipus?"

YEHUDA: The child's conflict within the love triangle. The conflict takes place either way.

ESTHER: So as far as you're concerned, that's the story? Making peace with love in a triangle in which my object of desire loves others besides me? Klein talks about jealousy toward the other two loving parties.

YEHUDA: It can be about a sibling, too. A child is part of a triangle and has to be okay with the idea that everybody loves everybody and everybody is in a rivalry with everybody. Lots of people can't be in a three-party relationship.

ESTHER: Correct.

YEHUDA: Because their Oedipus is unresolved.

ESTHER: I'm trying to get a precise answer from you about this Oedipal model, because just like other basic psychoanalytic concepts, the more basic the concept, the more confusing the meaning. This concept has at least three meanings I know of, three meanings that don't necessarily go together. It isn't just "everybody loves everybody," but "there are two other people who love each other, not just me." To the best of my knowledge, the main point is the difference between jealousy and envy, Klein's two distinct terms. The developmental task in the Oedipal phase is to acknowledge the fact that there are other couples in this triangle, ones I'm not a part of. In fact, it's more than a triangle, since you've brought the siblings into it, so you're saying it exists far beyond the triangle, in every relationship that involves more than two people.

YEHUDA: That is one of the elements of Oedipus: Mother has other objects besides me.

ESTHER: Mother has other love-objects besides me.

YEHUDA: Indeed, that's what allows me to break free without being rejected.

ESTHER: How come? There's rejection here.

YEHUDA: No. Rejection is something I manufacture when Mother won't release me. The experience of rejection – what happens when a person puts themselves in a state of humiliation or distress for being rejected – is not what happens following rejection in the real world. It's a manufactured fantasy, which causes the person to actually feel that way. Why must they fantasize about rejection? Because they were not rejected. If they truly had been rejected, if their mother actually told them, "Sweetheart, I've got a career, you aren't the only thing in my life, and you'd better learn to accept that," they would be released without feeling rejected. They'd be set free.

ESTHER: They would say, "All right, I'll move on and get my own career and my own life."

YEHUDA: "Thank goodness I don't always have to satisfy my mother's needs. Thank goodness there's somebody else to take my place while I'm gone."

Note

1 Bion, Wilfred R. (1984) *Transformations*. London: H. Karnac Books Ltd.

Reference

Bion, Wilfred R. (1984) *Transformations*. London: H. Karnac Books Ltd.

Chapter 7

Being Important or Rejected

This chapter will discuss what is concealed behind the prevalent experience of rejection. Or: how being rejected is being set free without asking for it.

We will discuss the combination of belonging (and therefore being important) and being humiliated (and therefore unimportant) – the masochistic combination. The deeper reason for the need to be rejected is to not belong, because belonging means, for many of us, losing our sense of subjectivity. The solution: Being important as an object, and knowing we have chosen this position as subjects.

ESTHER: This conversation will revolve around the dialectics of being rejected. This is a continuation of the previous chapter, in which we discussed Oedipus, and identified the experience of rejection as a solution for the problem of being too important to one's mother, without a father functioning as a regulator and barrier. This is the masochistic dialect, and it's common. Since many people suffer from feeling rejected, I'd like to dig deeper. In the previous chapter we concluded that being rejected means being free, but I think I haven't fully grasped the following equation:

Consciously rejected = Unconsciously free

I think clinical examples might be useful. Perhaps it's because the experience of those rejected is so convincing that I'm having difficulty viewing it as a solution. Here's an example:

A fifty-five-year-old woman, divorced and raising her only son, herself the only daughter of elderly parents who had her in their forties. She was an only child because her older brother died at war. This is a woman born into bereavement. Naturally or unnaturally, she took on a caretaking role from an early age. Her father was self-employed and worked long hours, and from the moment she was old enough to stand up, she took care of her mother. I'm mentioning this because I think it's connected to what she is going through with her son, who is thirty-two, married, and a father of two boys. Her relationship with him is the background to her seeking treatment.

DOI: 10.4324/9781003342458-7

I'd like to add one more thing about her: She's smart, quick, and sharp-witted, but she likes to give the impression that she isn't very knowledgeable. It takes a while to realize she's an intelligent person. She works at a low-level office job even though she is highly educated.

She claims that her son "takes care of his wife." His wife is a doctoral student and doesn't have a job. He coddles her, protects her, and makes sure she can do as she pleases. This son has high demands of his mother when it comes to her grandchildren. She comes over twice a week after work to take care of the kids so that her son can work and his wife can study. She brings them over to her place every other weekend, to let her son and his wife rest. The son has a lucrative sales business, and he and his family live an affluent lifestyle.

Now my patient's car is on its last legs, and recently she decided to buy a new one and asked her son for a loan. His response was, "You're such a failure. You don't know how to save money. When you divorced Dad, you didn't get any money from him, so now you're asking me?" That's what he said, those words, very aggressive. Like I said, the guy has plenty of money, and his mother takes care of his children, and she does it well, making sure they have everything they need, and she does it generously, and this is how he talks to her. In this case, the masochistic stance is clear. It's obvious, how she constitutes an object for him, and, in my opinion, how he turns her into an object by not treating her like a subject. For example, she says he never asks her how she's doing. She simply can't face him and tell him, "Don't talk to me that way" or "you don't respect me." She can't confront him with the fact that, in reality, he depends on her much more than she does on him. It's a pure masochistic dynamic.

Additionally, this woman is having a prolonged affair with a married man. On the one hand, I'm glad to know she has other relationships beyond this unhappy one with her son. On the other hand, having a relationship with a married man while she is unmarried is a relationship in which she is pining and longing. So, I see how she positions herself as rejected, but I can't see the gain, the solution this situation has to offer. You're saying "rejected means free" or "rejected means separate," and I don't see that here.

YEHUDA: When her son talks to her that way she isn't rejected, she's humiliated.

ESTHER: Yes, that's true.

YEHUDA: If she were rejected, she'd be free of humiliation.

ESTHER: That's the part I don't understand.

YEHUDA: The rejected doesn't belong, but the humiliated *does* belong. They are owned.

ESTHER: You're making a distinction between the rejected and the masochistic.

YEHUDA: The sadist owns their victim. Their victim belongs to them. But the rejected belongs to no one, and is therefore free from ownership. They are excluded from the group. Consider a pack of wolves: this pack has a leader, and the weakest link, through which the leader demonstrates its power. The weakest link belongs in the pack, by virtue of its relationship with the leader.

ESTHER: Okay, so that's her.

YEHUDA: On the other hand, there is the lone wolf, which isn't part of the pack.

ESTHER: Right. The rejected is on the outside, not belonging, but the humiliated belongs.

YEHUDA: Now, this humiliated one may want to be rejected. Being rejected might be preferable to being humiliated.

ESTHER: Okay.

YEHUDA: And here comes another twist: the third type here, other than the rejected and the humiliated, is important. The important is the one who bears the burden. This woman is very important to her son, as you've mentioned. Being important and being humiliated go together. He needs her; therefore, he owns her. By virtue of being important to him, he becomes her owner. The free person is one who has given up their importance.

ESTHER: But the free person isn't necessarily rejected. Can one be unimportant yet not rejected?

YEHUDA: We are discussing those who have set themselves free by leading themselves to be rejected. They become free by giving up their importance. Being important means bearing responsibility, because it means mattering to others. Some are lucky enough to free themselves without losing their importance and positioning themselves as rejected. In those cases, the father played the part of the barrier, and the child became beloved but not rejected by the mother, and separate by switching over to the father. The opposite of important is redundant. If the child consciously refused to be redundant, they unconsciously engineered a situation of being rejected. That way, they became redundant not by their own definition but by another's.

ESTHER: Yes.

YEHUDA: In the absence of a father, being rejected means stepping out of the role that is so important to others, and being free.

ESTHER: That's fascinating, because you're talking about life in a group, too. The way these mechanisms structure the position of an individual within a group.

YEHUDA: Now, this is all fantasy of course. Each of us decides for ourselves whether we are important or rejected. We can also generate scenarios in which others play along and reject us.

ESTHER: Unconsciously.

YEHUDA: Unconsciously. We can make it happen in practice, but that doesn't matter as much. It matters how we like to think of ourselves. I like to think of myself as someone indispensable, and therefore I collapse under the burden. It goes together. If someone tells me, "No worries, you can be replaced," I wouldn't be too thrilled to give up my burden.

ESTHER: You'd be insulted.

YEHUDA: That's right, I want to be important. On the other hand, there are some situations where I can't give up my desire to be important but still need a solution to set myself free. So I'll develop feelings of rejection. For example, if I don't feel like calling a friend then I'll be insulted because he didn't call me, either. I position myself as rejected in order to conceal the fact that I'm setting myself free.

ESTHER: Free from what?

YEHUDA: I'm not actually interested in being in touch, so I pretend to be insulted by him pulling away. I position myself as rejected when in fact I'm shedding my burden and putting it on him. I'm an insulted rejected, he's a guilty abandoner, and since it's his fault, I'm dismissed of any responsibility for our relationship. When couples need space from each other, their fights often take this form. It's another way of understanding how the person setting themselves free pretends – mostly to themselves – to be rejected.

ESTHER: I see.

YEHUDA: There's a developmental context, which we discussed in the previous chapter: When do we first come across this? When a child is too important to their mother. So important that the mother doesn't recognize them as separate, as a subject, a person in their own right, and there is no father to help set them free. The child cannot see themselves as a chooser and set themselves free, because in their own eyes they are not a subject capable of choice. Painting a picture of rejection is the only way. That's the foundation of masochism, and I think that's what's going on with your patient.

ESTHER: This is where I get stuck. Again, you're saying, painting a picture of rejection is the foundation of masochism. In that case, being rejected and being humiliated become the same thing.

YEHUDA: It depends on what the message is. If you tell someone, "You're not important and not useful," they think, "I'm free," because being unimportant is being free.

ESTHER: So there you go, her son told her, "You're worthless."

YEHUDA: "And who takes care of you and your children? Aren't I important as a caretaker?"

ESTHER: Okay, but she can't tell him that, that's the thing.

YEHUDA: Because she doesn't want to give it up! She could have told him, "You know what?"

ESTHER: "If this is how you treat me, I'm out of here!"

YEHUDA: "If I'm really so worthless and useless, then I don't matter as a caretaker. You can do without me." By saying that she's putting herself in a position where her son can't live without her.

ESTHER: True.

YEHUDA: And that makes her very important. I would ask her if she's willing to give up her importance to him. Because as long as she won't give it up, she'll be a victim of his humiliation. She could have told him, "You and your wife can figure things out on your own. I'll come back only if you show me some respect." She'd probably win that argument.

ESTHER: I'm sure she would.

YEHUDA: She doesn't want to.

ESTHER: Why doesn't she want to? That's what I'm trying to understand.

YEHUDA: She should tell her son, "I'm willing to give up being important, but are you willing to give up my help?" But she isn't willing to give up being important.

The masochist holds on to both things at once. Masochism is paradoxical because the masochist holds onto the freedom and the importance at once. Being a valuable object and simultaneously thrown out is the masochistic position. And that's what she is to her son, and perhaps to her parents as well. She's free because she's rejected but important because she's still needed.

ESTHER: I don't understand this definition of "free," Yehuda. Let's talk about this for a moment. How is she free, exactly?

YEHUDA: For example, she's free when she doesn't reveal her intelligence. She is free of the responsibilities she would have if she revealed that one could rely upon her intellectual abilities.

ESTHER: The interesting thing is, she isn't angry, she's insulted. And mostly, she identifies with what her son is saying, as if she lives her life believing she is worthless and powerless.

YEHUDA: This isn't a rejected stance, it's a humiliated stance. The rejected is the one who thinks, "I'm not accepted" or "I wasn't invited."

ESTHER: That isn't her. She says, "They don't want me," but she caused them not to want her. She looks – well, actually, you can hardly see her at all. She's very thin and unkempt. She practically hides her beauty.

YEHUDA: "And why do you make sure not to be wanted?" So I can remain free. "Why not entice them by telling them you'll do fine without them?" Because I have no choice. I can only make them choose to reject me, and then I'll be free.

ESTHER: That's true, she actually says, "I have no choice."

YEHUDA: That's masochism. That's the way we lead the other party to choose to set us free because they don't need us. So, her lover leaves her house in the middle of the night because he doesn't need her, so he sets her free. And if he wanted her so much that he chose to stay, she'd find another lover who didn't want her.

ESTHER: But what is her interest here?

YEHUDA: Her interest is to be free of any role, of being important to anyone.

ESTHER: Because?

YEHUDA: Because otherwise she's an object, she doesn't exist, she's someone else's plaything. It's a way to stop being an object used by another, when one cannot choose to leave.

This is a paradox. Actually, it's more than a paradox – it's a trap. It's a person with the developmental level of an object. Someone who never really separated from her mother and therefore doesn't see herself as having choice. Since she doesn't think she has choice she cannot choose to be free, but she is developed enough to crave freedom. In order to be free, she has to construct a scenario where freedom happens, but not by her initiation. It's like someone who can't just quit their job, so they get themselves fired. How? They mess up here, rile things up there, and choose the kinds of bosses who won't tolerate this behavior. That way they can supposedly be free without choosing it.

ESTHER: Okay. Now, for my benefit and our readers', can you clarify – is this because when this person becomes important to another, they believe that turns them into an object?

YEHUDA: Yes. Yes. Yes.

ESTHER: When they are in a relationship, they lose their sense of subjectivity.

YEHUDA: That's exactly right. They lose their sense of subjectivity. What happens to a more developed person is that they can be an object when they're important to another without losing their sense as a subject choosing this position.

ESTHER: Yes. Yes. People trip themselves up in all sorts of ways over the sense of loss of subjectivity. When they feel that, as a result of some relationship or another, be it professional or intimate, that they have become objects.

YEHUDA: Some people lead themselves to be rejected in order to be fired from their jobs, released without choosing it, since they can't choose to quit their jobs because they won't get severance pay, and they pull this maneuver consciously.

ESTHER: Yes.

YEHUDA: But right now, I'm talking about people who do it unconsciously, and therefore continue to feel rejected.

ESTHER: Right.

YEHUDA: And that is the complaint they bring with them to treatment, and so the purpose of the treatment becomes to show them how they themselves had created this rejection scenario.

ESTHER: Yes. And again: why can't they choose to quit?

YEHUDA: A prerequisite for choice – including the choice to retire, resign, or get some distance – is to be a subject with a right to choose. A prerequisite for existing as a subject is separation from one's mother. And there's the catch. Those who never separated from their mothers and therefore do not exist as subjects can only be released if somebody else, a different subject, chooses to release them. The person releasing them fills the function of separation, a function the person themselves cannot perform because they aren't yet a separate creature of choice.

ESTHER: So being dumped is being free? Doesn't being free mean being a choosing subject?

YEHUDA: Yes. But we're talking about those who can't be subjects, meaning, they can't take on responsibility for their own choices. If they were subjects to begin with, they would say, "I don't need to be rejected in order to be free, I'm free by virtue of my awareness that I choose to be here." Since they see themselves as someone without a choice, belonging means being trapped. Leaving is impossible too, because only those who can choose can choose to leave. So, I'll only be free if I get dumped. What does the patient you described gain from her relationship with the married lover or the son who abuses her? The forceful, controlling relationship makes her belong. Being someone's object is a way of belonging. The fact that someone has a right to hurt me emphasizes the fact that I'm their property. Part of this negative attitude is also rejection, and therefore release and dismissal from responsibility.

ESTHER: Good. Now let me share another case. This is a patient who excels in her free profession. Here's a story she told me at one of our first sessions, and which she defined as "formative" and seems relevant to this discussion of rejection as the path to freedom. Early on in her adult life, this woman worked as an employee at a company and had a very bad time. I think her suffering was very reasonable: Low salary, lots of hours, and so on. Most of her time on the job, she felt, to use her words, like she was being raped. Raped to work for too many hours for too little pay, raped to do things she felt were utterly wrong. She told her coworkers that she was in agony and was quite vocal in her criticism of the workplace. At the same time, she was a serious worker and did a good job, which was obvious to everybody around her. In short, she inspired an ambivalent attitude toward her – respect for her good work and discomfort with regard to her criticism and reservations. Finally, after two difficult years, she announced she was quitting.

At the end of her second year working there – shortly after she announced she was quitting – the colleagues had a party. This group of forty educated, polite people, as she put it, sat together on the balcony of the boss's house, and played a game. Each person in turn told someone why they liked them. Then that person had to tell someone else. Like a chain of affection. There are forty people in the group, so we're talking about three hours of this activity. She remembers well that she was the fourth to last person. "I was the fourth to last!" she said. "I've never been in this kind of situation before. It's hard to get over that kind of insult." But now I knew she herself had created this situation.

YEHUDA: When she told you this story, she referred to her time at that job as "rape."

ESTHER: Yes.

YEHUDA: So of course, she'd want to be free.

ESTHER: Right!

YEHUDA: I would have also preferred to be fourth to last to be raped than to be the first.

ESTHER: Right, it's better to be the fourth to last to be raped!

YEHUDA: Everybody is being raped, but it's better to be raped fourth to last than first.

ESTHER: One still has a chance to escape.

YEHUDA: Right. The first person to be raped is the most important, the most attractive. People want to abuse them the fastest.

ESTHER: Yes.

YEHUDA: The redundant person isn't worth abusing.

ESTHER: Right. That's how she felt, that she was being abused.

YEHUDA: Exactly. Now: she was insulted by being fourth to last because she was denying her choice. The other part of her, the part that wasn't insulted, is the part that is glad for getting their way, getting free. She wasn't trapped there for life.

ESTHER: So that's the story! That's the story of the free and rejected!

YEHUDA: Indeed.

Chapter 8

Orphanhood and Theology

This chapter will discuss Esther's difficulty in writing a lecture about orphanhood in the spirit of Lacanian thought; her doubts concerning the postmodern premise about the negation of God's existence; and about the solution we found in conversation: God as abstract object of desire, allowing a longing that isn't limited to a final object, thus creating the desiring subject.

ESTHER: I'm about to give a lecture at Haifa University, named "A Father without a Father."[1] It was obvious to me that my lecture would be founded on our first chapter, about orphanhood and solidarity. But as I prepared the lecture, some questions came up. I started writing, and instantly produced several pages about the experience of orphanhood, the direct encounter with the Real, and trauma. That's the first thing I wrote, and it's something I understand deeply, so the writing flowed. The lecture came out written almost like prose, and I felt comfortable with that. But then I stopped feeling so free. That happens to me sometimes, when I'm writing something that's less rooted in my lived experience. This happened when I reread our first chapter, about parenting that refuses to allow a teenager the illusion of authority. You discussed the solidarity that can exist between a parent and a child regarding their shared orphanhood, neither of them having someone to tell them what to do, an authority to tower over them, knowing best who they are and what they ought to do. In actuality, the chapter focuses on the specific aspect of parenting, the role of the one who is put in a position of authority. And that – the wish to hold onto the illusion of an authority who tells me what to do – is actually a wish to defend against the principle of universal orphanhood. So I wrote that, and I understand it, and it's easy, it's completely decipherable, and yet I felt blocked, the writing didn't flow, and I felt a kind of resistance. I don't think my resistance is entirely subjective, and it has at least two aspects. One of them is subjective. Let me put it this way: I found myself playing an obvious, banal, too-easy role of representing the secular-liberal position, because this is what the secular, western perception actually says: "Let's make a pact of solidarity because we all have a shared problem: there is no God." That's the

DOI: 10.4324/9781003342458-8

foundation of modern western culture. And I found myself representing this cliché, this consensus of modernism.

YEHUDA: That's the French Revolution: the king is dethroned, and the values that replace the monarchy reflect solidarity. This is also the message of Freud's *Totem and Taboo*: we kill the primordial father and erect a constitution in his place. So it's much deeper than liberalism.

ESTHER: I disagree. I think it's the modern, liberal interpretation of history.

YEHUDA: I think in this sense the very first liberal was Muhammad. He dismantled family rule, canceling the exclusive, omnipotent position of the father, and replacing the patriarchal family structure with religious solidarity, which features a different father figure.

ESTHER: Exactly, a hell of a father figure.

YEHUDA: But it's no longer familial, and that's already a step away from the imaginary nature of the patriarchy. And even earlier – Constantine, the Byzantine emperor, made a similar move when he turned the priest into a father, which is another way of weakening the family father. And so on and so forth, until modern liberalism weakened the religious father. But it's a movement that began ever earlier and started by weakening the status of the familial father.

ESTHER: So, like I said, I wrote a lecture, and a good one at that. I had to fill forty minutes, which usually poses no challenge for me, but what I wrote only took thirty minutes to read, and that was a sign of lack of vitality. Because I was expressing an idea, I wasn't totally comfortable with, and it happened twice. There was one paragraph I wrote and deleted because it seemed simplistic, and another one, where I said that the "solidarity of orphans" is the foundation of liberal perception, and I added that this wasn't an easy position to hold, and that's the kernel of what I want to discuss with you. I said it was a difficult position to hold because it is faced with other, much stronger forces. I compared it to an encounter between a child whose father is dead (representing secular liberalism) and a child whose father is alive (representing current-day Islam), and said children who had a strong father who told them what to do have an easy time fighting children who don't have a father. I'd pointed at a certain weakness of liberalism – a weakness resulting from being an orphan, because not having a father weakens a person in one way or another. I have one patient whose story I told in order to describe orphanhood: his father died when he was four years old, and the child's symptoms started with hyperactivity during his first years at school. Now he's almost forty, and he came to treatment immediately following the birth of his eldest son. His central symptom these days is a difficulty in executing his ambitions. As I wrote, I realized I came up with something very structured, very symptomatically cohesive: he would spend a period of time thinking about starting a specific business. He had a clear idea in mind. And believe me, if he put his mind to it, he could get it done. The guy was smart, educated, and had all the necessary tools. He was responsible and methodical and had a vision. In other words, he should have no problem starting a business.

YEHUDA: He didn't have the desired mechanism he was supposed to have inherited from his father.

ESTHER: Okay, and then – hang on, listen to the whole story – he would go see people he respects, people with know-how and experience, and ask their advice about his business idea. He kept coming up with different ideas, not because he gave up on the previous idea, but because somehow, magically, everyone always discourages him from his initiatives. Don't bother, forget it, it won't work . . . As far as I understand, the advice he gets is un-paternal, in the sense that they are discouraging. See? His symptom isn't instability or impotence, but his reliance on others, others that are always, in essence, non-fathers, hoping to get something they can't give him, because they are his non-fathers. This is an actual symptom: creating the presence of a father in his death, in his absence. Creating his presence by creating his absence, by turning to everyone who isn't his father and getting their non-father, negative responses.

YEHUDA: I see him turning to another in the hopes of receiving the right answer. There are two answers he could receive that are the wrong answers. One is, "Leave me alone, I'm not your father, I can't take responsibility for you, I can't make your decision for you. And if you insist on taking my advice, then my advice is don't do it, because I don't want to take any paternal responsibility for you."

ESTHER: Yes, that's what happens to him.

YEHUDA: Another wrong answer might be, "Sure, you want me to give you directions? Here you go: do these three things." And then your patient has to admit the truth to himself: no one can actually tell him what to do, so again it doesn't work. The answer he needs is, "I'm sorry you don't have a father."

ESTHER: Right. And so, in a way, I wasn't comfortable with my theory. So, let's move from this specific case to the theory, because the story is very clear, but that's just the thing, you see? You can't live without a father.

YEHUDA: You can.

ESTHER: Hang on, wait, because I'm trying to make a theology. What I'm getting at is: you can't live without God.

YEHUDA: Okay.

ESTHER: I'm trying to say that killing God is too simple. Too simple, you see?

YEHUDA: Just because the big Other doesn't exist doesn't mean we shouldn't use it.

ESTHER: No, no, no, I know that idea, you've told me that already. That isn't enough for me.

YEHUDA: Fine, then believe in God.

ESTHER: This isn't about belief. That's why I told you there's nothing neurotic about my resistance. I have no need and no belief, but I don't think everything starts and ends with need, meaning – with desire and *jouissance*. In your theory, desire is the predicate, the basic assumption, and the only starting point. I find that limited –

YEHUDA: You're saying you don't want to take God out of the picture.

ESTHER: I can't. I can't.

YEHUDA: Then don't.

ESTHER: No, listen. It's funny and graceful, the way you're locking me inside a circular argument. But when you do that, it puts an end to our discussion, because you're attributing me with a subjectivity that is different than yours by definition, and that leaves no foundation for our discourse.

YEHUDA: That's just it: believe in whatever suits you.

ESTHER: That response is exactly where the problem lies: with this endless generosity that allows me to believe whatever I choose but does not allow for non-subjective discourse on a matter too great to be reduced to "need" or "desire."

YEHUDA: No, the discussion doesn't end, because when I tell you to go ahead and do what you want, believe what you want, that does something to you –

ESTHER: You're wrong, it doesn't do something to me, it does something to the discussion – it ends it.

YEHUDA: You're saying you don't want to end the discussion.

ESTHER: That's right.

YEHUDA: I'm not saying this in order to end the discussion. I'm saying this so you can say, "I don't want to end the discussion" and I can ask, "why?" and then we can continue the discussion in a deeper way. Why don't you want to end the discussion?

ESTHER: Mostly because it really isn't deep enough, but rather circular, and therefore blocked. Saying "believe whatever you want" whenever the question of God comes up is uncommunicative. Earlier, you said that the French Revolution, the Prophet Muhammad, and Constantine the Great all worked against the patriarchy. The real father, the father of the family, had to be dethroned. Maybe we can narrow the discussion to the cultural-developmental importance of dethroning the father and avoid rising all the way up to God. If we want a real discussion, why should we talk about God?

YEHUDA: In that case, we have to be practical. Meaning, we have to ask which God we're getting rid of and which one we're keeping, which function of His we have to give up, and which we can keep.

ESTHER: Correct.

YEHUDA: Because the word "God" in and of itself isn't important. What we have to define is the godly function that disrupts development.

ESTHER: The function we need to discuss is personal providence.

YEHUDA: So, this is the God we're getting rid of – personal providence. We get to keep the God of pantheism, of Spinoza . . . Why not? Nature is beautiful and functional –

ESTHER: No, you're being cynical.

YEHUDA: And it's got a fabulous architecture . . . but personal providence is exactly the idea of the missing mother and father. The thing that solidarity replaces. It's the thing missing from perfection – the promise that everything is going to be all right. That's personal providence.

ESTHER: Yes.

YEHUDA: There is no promise that everything is going to be all right. There's a promise that everything isn't going to be all right. Meaning, there's a structural flaw.

ESTHER: Excellent.

YEHUDA: And that is the basis for solidarity: the fact that we all have a structural flaw. And the only reason that any God ever existed here is that He is the exception that proves the rule. And the rule is that we are all lacking.

It goes like this: first, Lacan said that the mind, or – more accurately – the unconscious – is structured like language. Later, he said: structured like logic. Finally, he just said: structured. The mind is a structure. A structure requires formulas, axioms, and logic. According to Seminar 20, there is male logic and female logic. Male logic is: there's the rule and the exception. The rule can be: all men wear a tux to special events; therefore, they are all the same. All men have a phallus, which defines them as part of a group. A man knows who he is by his group affiliation, the place where everyone shares his qualities. The phallus they share makes them the same. This is, in fact, castration. Meaning, the existing possibility of not having it. Meaning, they all share a lack. A logical structure is needed for defining the lacking as opposed to the whole, and that's what God was invented for.

ESTHER: He is the whole.

YEHUDA: Right. Here is the whole that none of us is; the whole that allows us to acknowledge our lack. The exception that structures the rule is the outlier that defines the limit of the group.

ESTHER: Right. It's an idea that exists in religious thought as well: the whole that emphasizes our lack.

YEHUDA: Exactly. God's function is to make us all orphans – orphans in the sense that we are missing something and have no one to correct that.

ESTHER: Okay.

YEHUDA: So, we replace the father that promises wholeness, the more primitive father, or perhaps the mother?

ESTHER: With a father that points to a lack and inspires desire.

YEHUDA: The father who promises a personal providence is the father who promises wholeness, as part of a belief in wholeness. But there's another father, and I'd say this is the father Rabbi Isaac Luria talked about, who is himself lacking – like in the reduction process: contraction, breakage, amending.

ESTHER: But know that He is lacking by choice.

YEHUDA: That's what he's like – lacking. And we who are made in His image are lacking as well. It's a variation of orphanhood, and it means that the father – God – does not exempt us from orphanhood. The orphanhood of the fantasy of wholeness. It is the antithesis of the fantasy of wholeness – the fantasy of someone who can make us whole. So, let's not talk in a simplifying way about whether there is or is no God, or whether there is or is no father, but about whether there is or is no father who promises wholeness.

ESTHER: I think what bothered me as I was writing the lecture was that I, by the act of writing, was not allowing the existence of God. I don't want to defend God's existence or prove it, but now I can allow the existence of a God who is neither a fundamentalist nor a sadist.

YEHUDA: And is Himself lacking.

ESTHER: And does not order anyone to kill in order to attain wholeness, but is Himself lacking, and lacking by choice. It's a different lack than ours.

YEHUDA: Indeed, this divine choice has significance. Because let's address the term "A father without a father" (the name of the lecture). Let's think about it not as a historical, traumatic event in which a person becomes orphaned as a child and now has a son, but as a representation of the father's stance that is derived from this event; his stance as a father without a father: he recognizes his own lack from within his own fatherhood. That's comparable to God's choice to contract Himself.

ESTHER: Excellent, now I understand you. That's a nice idea, but we aren't finished yet. There is another paternal contraction I'd like to address: the reduction of the God that decided to tell Abraham not to sacrifice Isaac. The Lacanian interpretation of the binding of Isaac deals with Abraham's unwillingness to give up the absolute father who tells everyone what to do. I almost used this in my lecture, but ultimately, I decided not to. Indeed, one of the versions claims that after Abraham was told to let the child go, he protested and suggested strangling the child instead. When the angel once again instructed him to let the child be, Abraham asked to at least draw some of his blood. But just because Abraham was told not to hurt the child doesn't mean he wasn't being ordered. He received a very clear order: not to hurt the child. In light of this, it would be wrong to assume the point is that he is willing to do anything for authority – or, in Lacanian interpretation, to do anything to keep the authority in place. The authority continues to exist. It tells him to leave the child alone. It does tell him what to do. You, as representative of Lacanian theory, cannot argue that Abraham wants to make the child bleed because he wants to preserve the idea of having someone tell him what to do. He was told what to do – the angel told him *not* to touch the child. So, what I'm saying is, Abraham isn't trying to force the existence of God's authority, because it already exists. God continues to give orders, and this time his order is not to do. Some orders are about doing and some orders are about not doing.

YEHUDA: Indeed, there is an order here, but the order is not a demand. There is a difference between an order and a demand. A demand, simply put, would be, "Give me something." See? "Take something away from yourself and give it to me."

ESTHER: Sacrifice, yes, okay.

YEHUDA: That's the beginning of authority, in the anal phase, when the parents demand that the child give away his poop and therefore be demanded and believe someone is making demands on them, thus experiencing the confidence that someone is there to manage them and protect them from their own drives. This is all founded on the demand, on something being taken away.

ESTHER: Yes.

YEHUDA: Now, being demanded *not* to give something, as Abraham is instructed in the story of the binding, creates a paradox. If I'm sophisticated enough, I can experience the wrath of the one who forbids me to give. But it's paradoxical. It isn't like experiencing the wrath of one who takes something away from me – be it my feces, my child, or my money. If God told him, "Do whatever you think, I'm not getting involved," He would have allowed Abraham to sacrifice his son to God. Abraham could have made this choice. But God thwarted this by intervening. If God said nothing, Abraham could have attributed the demand to him.

ESTHER: Why? I don't understand.

YEHUDA: If Abraham said, "Please, let me just make him bleed a little," and God didn't answer, that would have allowed Abraham to make his son bleed.

ESTHER: Or not.

YEHUDA: Correct. He might have chosen the positive act of strangling or bleeding. God didn't want to allow him to delude himself that there was someone expecting these gifts, so He said, "I won't accept them."

ESTHER: Do you realize we've just switched from an atheistic model to a theological-developmental model?

YEHUDA: Yes. That you can have a God, it just depends on what kind.

ESTHER: Precisely. Believe it or not, but you just participated in an anti-agnostic act. You said, "God, but not that kind of God." You're saying, not a sadistic God, not an anal God, not a God to whom you give something only to feel like God removed it from you and now owes you one for as long as you live, and not a God who chooses for you or pushes you to be whole and flawless. I call this "a theological-developmental model" in the spirit of Maimonides. Maimonides always tried to lift up faith, lift up worship, higher and higher each time, higher than the mental need for faith, than the need for authority and the need for an illusion of endless good and personal providence – meaning, the illusion of protection. He wanted people to open their eyes, see clearly, and rise up without their emotional needs, in whose image they designed their God's image. Finally, one reaches a thought model, which, if you please, Yeshayahu Leibowitz took to the extreme. Leibowitz was originally a follower of Maimonides, and is a profound negativist who refuses to attribute God with any title or form. Put simply, his claim is that nothing can be said about God, which leaves the Jewish believer with the pure choice to actualize his act of faith – the mitzvahs. So, one might say Leibowitz was a borderline heretic.

YEHUDA: At this point, I'd like to take things one step further. There's a God who approves, or allows, or orders there to be no authority.

ESTHER: That there is no anal God, and no banal God.

YEHUDA: God himself announces, "Ladies and Gentlemen, there is no authority!" And we believe Him, because He's authoritative, and we stop believing in authority. It's still a paradox. That's a problem.

ESTHER: A paradox is not a problem. A paradox is absolutely not a problem. A paradox is wonderful; it's reality. Reality is a paradox.

YEHUDA: Hang on. The psychoanalytic experience tries to move past this. The psychoanalyst doesn't inform their patient, "Listen, there is no authority, trust me, I know what I'm talking about." Instead, they let patients talk until they figure it out on their own. That's why the analyst doesn't try to take God's place or the father's place. They don't try to offer personal providence or promise a corrective experience, nor do they instruct their patients to despair. Only the subject's statement counts, which means we can move beyond the God that allows us not to believe. We can stop believing without getting permission from the authority.

ESTHER: Right. That's what the Buddhists do. Or, you could say they do the opposite: they believe without getting permission from the authority.

YEHUDA: This, then, is about a third developmental stage: at first, we believe in a demanding God, then in a God that refuses to demand and therefore apply his authority, and later we give up on Him and realize there is no authority.

ESTHER: Let's turn to Zen Buddhism, shall we? That would be more convenient than Judaism, because it isn't monotheistic thought. In the essence of Buddhist thought, there is no image or persona, no creating God. Now, that isn't completely accurate. People can't make it without an image, and that's one of the reasons I wanted us to talk about the matter of "no-father," because a person cannot be wholeheartedly orphaned, cannot avoid missing the God figure. So instead of God – because there is no metaphysics in Buddhism; the Buddha refused to deal with metaphysics – they turned the Buddha into a God. They made a fifteen-meter-high golden Buddha statue, all while the Buddha himself had no intention of being anyone's father and certainly not anyone's God, but there he was, made into a God. You see?

In non-monotheistic so-called "theologies" you find a different phenomenon: historical figures are divined, reframed as gods. This is the case for Lao-Tze and Confucius in China. It's different than what happens in monotheistic religions, but not necessarily better. Judaism is considered the first monotheistic system of thought for defining a single God, thus indicating unity rather than divergence. To force us to stick to this one, eternal God, Judaism turned divinity into an abstract concept that's hard to grasp. The second commandment is "Thou shalt not make unto thee any graven image," denouncing any objectification of God. Thus, any projection of a father figure derived from emotional needs – the authoritative father on the one hand; the protective father on the other – crashes against a wall. It isn't this, it isn't that, it isn't any single namable quality. Neither father nor personal providence. This God is our father who art in heaven, but that's merely a sentimental name, which does not appear in the original scripture.

Now, to step out of monotheism, in Zen thought, whenever you veer into metaphysics by referring to some existence beyond the here and now, it counts as a descent of the clear mind – a descent into delusion. In short, different theologies have strong thought models (what I'm doing right now would be a faux-pas in Buddhism – calling Zen and Buddhism "theologies"). Strong thought models whose function is to prevent, really move people away from the mental habit of getting stuck in utilitarian perceptions of God by outfitting Him with some function or another according to their emotional needs. Usefulness, or functionality, means projecting onto the image of God: believing it demands something of you, benefits you, protects you, or embraces you – all those functions Christianity nurtures with its Holy Trinity and that monotheism in general promotes. Those models mostly demand evolvement, because they pull you out of this image of God we look for in different circumstances, according to our emotional state. What I'm saying right now is the exact opposite of the basic requirement of your theory. It's anti-usefulness; the opposite of usefulness. It's charming, and it subverts the basic assumption of God's functionality.

YEHUDA: Why do we need a God if not to use Him?

ESTHER: "Use Him" – fantastic! But as far as I'm concerned, this is the end of the discussion. It's an excellent question. You're going to say, "I don't need God, so God is gone," and I'll say, "God exists or does not exist regardless of whether or not you need Him." That's the absolute. Your consciousness – human consciousness in general – due to its structure, cannot perceive anything that lacks purpose. That's true, but this consciousness does have a different interesting capability – it can perceive the absolute. You use the terms "whole" and "perfect," which are functional. You can say, "Humans perceive the whole in order to derive from it the lacking." So I'm saying: not whole, but absolute. There is no emotional connotation to the term "absolute." It isn't perfection, it's something you cannot understand, okay?

YEHUDA: It's the Real.

ESTHER: Yes, from a certain perspective it's the Real.

YEHUDA: Lacan said that one of the synonyms for "Real" is "impossible." He said Freud's Real was the occult, because it was interesting but also heresy. We could place God as the Real – meaning, the impossible for an atheist. If an atheist says there is no God, they are placing God in a negative stance, meaning, the impossible, the Real.

ESTHER: But I – and I'm not a heretic, nor am I an atheist, exactly – I'm also placing God in a position where it's impossible to know Him, and so for me, He is also in the Real and the impossible, but without denying His existence.

YEHUDA: Okay. And then the only reason for His existence is your choice.

ESTHER: That is the heretic view.

YEHUDA: It's your choice to believe in the absolute.

ESTHER: I don't choose to believe in the absolute, I just have no idea.

YEHUDA: You just believe in the absolute?

ESTHER: I don't "believe" in anything. I *don't know*. The difference between us is that I don't know. And that's a huge difference. Enormous. That's the difference, and that's all it takes as far as I'm concerned. The entire difference between us is that you're forcing yourself to deal with "is" and "isn't" while I just say, "I don't know." And as soon as I say, "I don't know," I'm leaving something open in my consciousness. Bion says, "Tolerance to doubt and a sense of infinity." I leave a spot open for doubt. I don't deal with faith. I'm not interested in faith. That isn't a living concept for me. I don't understand it. I deal with doubt, with the possibility of a mind open to doubt, and this openness allows me to cast doubt on the theory of desire that is the foundation of everything; the desire that Lacan defined as the cornerstone of existence. What if that's wrong? What if it isn't desire that is the foundation? Why not leave the question open? It's so close-minded: desire, the purpose and function of every limb of existence . . .

YEHUDA: But I'm still searching for the function.

ESTHER: I know, but maybe you can stop looking for it. You're wasting your life searching for functions. That's why you're secular – you keep looking for functions.

YEHUDA: That name – God – what's the significance of the existence or nonexistence of the thing behind the signifier?

ESTHER: Well, that's a good question. That's what we ought to be dealing with.

YEHUDA: And when I say "significance" I'm saying "function," but I'm also asking if there is any significance *beyond* function. If we can identify that thing, we can conclude what the purpose of this whole endeavor is. So let's go straight there.

ESTHER: Yes, that happened to me too, because of your enlightened influence. All sorts of things happen, driving me more or less out of my mind. That's fabulous, but hang on, what time is it? Do we still have time?

YEHUDA: We've still got time to go out of our minds, yes.

ESTHER: Yes, I don't mind going out of my mind, happy to, you have no idea. Since I've started studying with you, I've become less religious. It's sweeping me away, but I still have that longing. Breslau Chassids talk about longing. Some people say that's the function – the longing.

YEHUDA: The desire, the address for desire.

ESTHER: Now, longing, I want to tell you, yes, lack, longing, lack and longing, desire – we understand all that. But why?

YEHUDA: Well, at this point, the more abstract God is, the better, because it isn't a longing for a specific thing.

ESTHER: Yes. Good. That also sits well with theological thought. What I'm trying to say is that this allows longing not for a partner, not for sex, not for children, not for a career, not –

YEHUDA: And not to think of this longing as a demand that can be fulfilled. There are different words that indicate variations on the object of desire. There is simple biological need. There is the drive for pleasure, which is derived of physical needs but also inspired by human society, which passes it on through stories. There is the demand, which is the attempt to gain confidence that our wishes will come true and we will be protected against frustration. What all these forms of desire share is that they are all aimed at a particular, definable object. Theoretically, there is an object assumed to allow satisfaction of these desires. Why do I say "theoretically?" Because if there is anything we can rely on in human experience, it is the persistence of the experience of lack, a lack of prolonging satisfaction. So, what is this desire that continues to pulse through us even after the demand for objects is satisfied? It is a desire not aimed at the receiving of an object. It's desire. Desire does not seek an object for satisfaction, but attests to the existence of the desiring subject. "I desire, therefore I am." The godly object is the northern star toward which our wishes are aimed, not in order to reach it, but to keep it existing, because it enables the existence of desire, which enables the existence of the subject.

ESTHER: Right.

YEHUDA: We are in the desire, period. Desire in its absolute form, without an object that could diminish it by satisfaction. God as a recipient of prayers is lacking, but an absolute recipient nonetheless. We aim our desires at Him, and He is lacking so that nothing can stop our desire.

ESTHER: I would leave God as the ultimate recipient, without re-negating or re-affirming his existence.

YEHUDA: I feel good about it.

ESTHER: Just like that.

YEHUDA: It's all good.

ESTHER: Fully open.

Note

1 Paper: "Father without a Father" Given on 2.1.2017 at a conference on "Love, Guilt and Amending" at the interdisciplinary clinical center of the faculty of welfare and health at Haifa University. The conference was in honour of a book by Amit Fechler "A Father without a Father: Love, Guilt and Amending in the life of people who are orphaned of their father".

Chapter 9

Real, Imaginary, and Symbolic

Lacan's Three Orders are: the Real, the Imaginary, and the Symbolic.

The human creature moves between its whole image, which is called "I," and the real experience. There is a relationship between these two – the Real and the Imaginary – and life in the Symbolic world. In the Symbolic world, this "I" receives different names: someone's father, someone's child, someone's sibling, someone's friend. These are names we can move between, thus living a dynamic life – neither static as in the Imaginary order nor chaotic as in the Real order.

ESTHER: I was charmed by something you said in our last session: that Lacan would have given up the Oedipal model for the sake of a purely structural model devoid of developmental content; one that deals with the structure of the mind. If I'm understanding correctly, this model is not obligated to content.

YEHUDA: Right, it's a logical model. He used the Oedipal model as an allegory, a metaphor, or perhaps a mythologizing of a logical principle. The principle is one of separation. The father castrates the mother or the child, and it's an interesting story, but the logic behind it deals with the question of whether things are connected or separate.

ESTHER: At the center of the Oedipal story is a dialectic of connection and separation.

YEHUDA: Yes.

ESTHER: Meaning, the remaining content is: to be a subject one must create a separation; to be a creature that is connected to their father, their mother, their siblings, but also separate from them all.

YEHUDA: Indeed. But, as we said, Lacan actually gave up this model, pointing to processes of separation and disconnection, and instead created a slimmer, more abstract theory that includes the three orders – the Symbolic, the Imaginary, and the Real. As far as he's concerned, different contents can be poured into this abstract triangle. Since the three orders necessarily work together, there is no single correct story, no single linear plot, because they work together and depend on each other, so even if I pave a developmental

DOI: 10.4324/9781003342458-9

path here – one that depicts what things look like for a baby, then a small child, then an adolescent, and so on – discussing them through a developmental model is just one possible route among many combinations. So, this developmental route begins with a child being born into the Real. Their body is not cohesive, they have no coordination, they feel themselves –

ESTHER: They don't "feel themselves" because there is no "self." They feel all sorts of things.

YEHUDA: They feel all sorts of things. The "self" does not yet exist, but something else exists that leads them to realize they are missing something, that there are older people who walk around them on two legs and speak of them as something that exists in the world. The baby doesn't feel themselves to be the thing they are discussing. They wonder, who is that they are referring to? When they say "sweetie," who do they mean? What gradually takes the place of the answer to the question of who they are is their mirror image. When they look in the mirror, they take on an outside perspective of themselves. They see themselves as others do – a whole. They think, Oh! That's me! I am the thing the others see. By being on the outside of themselves, they can see themselves and know they exist. But this act is a kind of exile, because as soon as a child takes on an outside perspective of themselves, they are exiled from themselves. This is an exchange: one can receive an existence, an identity, an understanding of who they are, perhaps even feel whole – because the mirror image has closed contours that create a single, whole figure – you can have this wonderful gift in exchange for exiling your soul.

ESTHER: Exiling it from what?

YEHUDA: The "I" comes at the expense of something.

ESTHER: I'm confused. Where does the soul exile from? That same chaotic experience of the Real?

YEHUDA: From the existence of the body. Not from the "self" but from the chaotic world of sensation. The child becomes "I," and "I" is about appearing rather than sensing. People who don't undergo this exile experience psychosis, because they have no outside perspective of themselves. To be more exact: they experience an outside perspective of themselves, the idea of watching themselves from the outside, as persecution. What they experience is chaotic; it's the pre-imaginary phase. It's the experience before the mirror phase, or in the middle of it, because the mirror phase is never complete. This is what happens in certain kinds of fragmentary psychoses. A psychotic patient once described his experience in the hospital. He said, "I want to tell you that the 'I' is not a given. Did you know it can fall apart, and then you stop being 'I'?" He had the experience that the contours in the mirror couldn't hold his whole image, the illusion of unity that we call "I."

ESTHER: A similar thing happens in meditation. In fact, this is a well-worn, somewhat banal comparison between the mystical experience and the psychotic one. It's wrong in many ways, but the true part of it is that in meditation one returns to the body. The basic instruction in meditation is not to think but to feel, to sense. It isn't about a forceful cancellation of thought, but in choosing sensation instead. Sometimes meditation guides suggest focusing on the area below the navel, which I believe is known as the Earth Chakra in Indian epistemology. Focusing on the area below the navel rather than on the head, where thoughts happen. It's about giving permission to pay attention to what enters through the senses, as well as to what emerges as a sensual experience. For instance, listening to one's heartbeat. Being completely open to experience. When one is fully open, one doesn't think, because thought is not experience, it's observing experience from the outside, like looking at oneself in the mirror. When that happens – when you are one with your experience rather than observing it from the outside through thought – that's happened to me a few times during meditation, and when it happens, the word "I" dies, becomes worthless. It has nothing to do with experience.

This experience is frightening at first, because the lines between you and the world disappear and you're busy feeling rather than delineating the sensation. But even though this description is reminiscent of psychosis, meditation has its own unique character.

YEHUDA: And there's another way to get there. It doesn't have to be through the developmental failure of psychosis. One can get there through trauma. Meaning, that even the most safely held person can experience a collapse of the Imaginary systems that hold them, such as witnessing a terrorist bombing and seeing body parts no longer connected to one cohesive image. The experience of trauma –

ESTHER: The experience of trauma is excellent in this sense.

YEHUDA: Why?

ESTHER: Speaking from my experience with myself and traumatic patients, they have an existential understanding that is on another dimension than for people who never experienced trauma. You could say they know the Real, know something about life that others don't.

YEHUDA: Yes.

ESTHER: In a way, they've tapped into the secret.

YEHUDA: They've seen the camera and realized they've been living in a movie.

ESTHER: Yes. And then they've got options. One option – the better one – is the opportunity for freedom. Trauma contains a developmental opportunity: since the Imaginary is shattered and there is no longer a certain, soothing illusion of who one is. Instead, there's a large range that didn't exist before. I have a patient whose child was sick and his life was in danger. The family was going through a period of uncertainty regarding the child's future, and the doctors couldn't offer any clear forecast. One day, things changed. The parents were told their child was no longer in danger. He began to recover, and now he's doing well. A few days after the doctor informed them that the child was no longer in danger, she came to our treatment session and told me about it. Then she said, "I'm a little dead." I asked her about that, and she said, "I met up with an ex-boyfriend I used to love so much, but I couldn't emotionally connect. The meeting was dull." On its face, this sounds trivial – trauma had diminished her ability to feel. But as we continued to speak, I found out that there was a hidden truth. She actually felt attracted to this guy. Now, she could panic – the ideal image of the wholeness of her life is shattered and now she's feeling things she hasn't felt in a long time, if ever. Perhaps, to hide this palpitating life that threatens her ideal picture of her current relationship, she started by saying, "I'm a little dead," when in fact this experience is a return to life. She said she loved her child much more intensely now, and it's all traumatic, all stemming from trauma, and all of a sudden, an experiential world that didn't exist before is opening up inside of her. She's living. It's natural to be afraid of this. Now she has to choose, to use your words, "to reenter the Imaginary and Symbolic "virtual" orders."

YEHUDA: That's right.

ESTHER: Now it's a matter of choice rather than a given state as it had been before the trauma. After the trauma, one has a choice, a different way in.

YEHUDA: Yes.

ESTHER: Entering by choice.

YEHUDA: Right, now she knows it's virtual and can choose how to participate. Before, she didn't know it was virtual.

ESTHER: Exactly.

YEHUDA: This virtuality is the Symbolic and the Imaginary. It's what Lacan calls the "sense," which he describes as "dual madness" – *folie a deux*. These two follies, the Imaginary and the Symbolic, join together to produce a reality. But in certain situations, such as trauma, this reality turns out to be a theatre. Choosing sense means turning trauma into tragedy.

ESTHER: Yes, trauma awakens one from the illusion of sense, or meaning. It dissolves it.

YEHUDA: But it doesn't create a different sense, it fragments it. Now let's return to the three orders: Real, Imaginary, and Symbolic. The child looks at his mirror image and thinks, oh, there I am! And at that moment, they are exiled from their inner experience to exterior identification. This is narcissism, and it's essential, because without it we experience severe psychotic phenomena, the deconstruction of the self. In traumatic situations, this imaginary structure, narcissism, can fall apart and regroup through the Symbolic. Now, what is the Symbolic order? When a baby looks at their mirror image, they need someone to validate what they're seeing. To tell them, yes, that's you. The parent does this, and that is the Symbolic order, the Symbolic operating system. The Symbolic operating system is branched, and its components depend on one another. A person depends on society just as a word's meaning depends on the sentence. The connection between a word and a sentence is contextual: we can use the word "coffee" in the context of "Can I please have a large coffee?" or in the context of "Would you like to come up for a cup of coffee?" The word would receive two very different meanings through its context. Subjects receive their meanings through social context. You can be someone's son, someone's father, someone's friend, and so on. The mirror freezes a person, and this stability is what's gained through identity, the identity received through the mirror image. But it comes at a price: in exchange for identity, one must freeze and go static. It's just like a long exposure photograph, where the subject must stay perfectly still. To have an image of yourself, you must keep perfectly still. Then how do you go back to movement? Do you go back to the chaotic movement of the Real? If you do that, you won't know who you are again. That's not a good idea. Luckily, there's another option – the Symbolic. You'll be identified with a word, but it'll have two meanings. You'll exist but also experience fluid boundaries with others. That is metonymy. Metonymy is the seeping of meaning from one word to another. I can be someone's father in one moment, someone's son in another moment, a psychoanalyst in another, or a student in another. None of these identities freezes me the way the mirror image does, but they do offer an existence. The Real is a deconstruction of the Imaginary-Symbolic illusory identity. The Symbolic reconciles the Imaginary and the Real.

ESTHER: The chaotic and the static.

YEHUDA: Precisely.

ESTHER: It's dynamic.

YEHUDA: True. The chaos is dynamic as well.

ESTHER: Indeed, at first, I wanted to say "between the dynamic and the static," but that isn't accurate. It's the bridge between the chaotically dynamic –

YEHUDA: Correct.

ESTHER: The Symbolic is the dynamic founded on logical causal order. It mediates the dynamic of the Real, which is chaotic –

YEHUDA: With the static existence of the imaginary image. You could say it's the best of both worlds. It takes the dynamic nature of the Real and the existence of the Imaginary. Now it's time to ask, what do we recommend? What are the ethics here? What's the right way to live with this? And there is an answer.

ESTHER: So, what you're saying is: we are born into the initial experience of chaos. In other words, we are born into the Real, in the sense that there is no image to our experience. That's what you've been saying as I understand it.

YEHUDA: Yes, for now. It's one of the ways to put the three orders in sequence.

ESTHER: Next, you said, we look in the mirror. Our mother picks us up, shows us ourselves in the mirror, and says, "That's you, my sweet child." And we say, Look at that! We've got an image, a clear form, a contour we can see through our eyes, not our ears, or our noses, or our hands –

YEHUDA: "Seeing" is a metaphor, because blind people also have the experience of a mirror image.

ESTHER: How can they?

YEHUDA: By being talked about and asking themselves who this person being talked about is.

ESTHER: So the mirror isn't an essential condition. The emphasis is on the combination: looking at the mirror while being told that what you're seeing is yourself. Without the words that accompany the mirror image, the process won't take place.

YEHUDA: Right.

ESTHER: Meaning, the act is Symbolic even when it comes through the Imaginary.

YEHUDA: Correct. We said we would first talk about all three orders separately, then see how they work in concert. We've also said this is just one possible path. We could have started with the Symbolic, say a person is born into a world in which the myth within which they will live is already written.

ESTHER: Let's say that, too.

YEHUDA: I'm saying: a person is born into a situation in which their name, their fate, and the desires of their predecessors are injected into their body through language. They have little wiggle room to decide what they can do with their preordained fate.

ESTHER: Poor us . . .

YEHUDA: The goal of treatment is to break free from all that as much as we can, in a way. Another aspect of treatment is to accept this fate, the fact that we cannot choose our words, the signifiers controlling us.

ESTHER: All right, so now we've started the story of creation from a different point, and this point tells us what we're born into. We're born into an order –

YEHUDA: A Symbolic order.

ESTHER: Too much order –

YEHUDA: Whether it's too much or not is attested by the symptom.

ESTHER: That's it!

YEHUDA: Not everyone comes to analysis. Not everyone undergoes treatment, and not everyone needs it. Some people live peacefully with the myth they were born into.

ESTHER: But it involves ignorance.

YEHUDA: Some people are born and die without ever peeking outside of the myth in which they live.

ESTHER: I know. They are truly ignorant.

YEHUDA: Right.

ESTHER: Wait, so if you say that some people live in peace with this myth, without any trouble or need for treatment, and that's okay, does that mean you don't uphold knowledge as a value in itself?

YEHUDA: No, I don't. I value healing.

ESTHER: Meaning, your basic value is a lack of suffering.

YEHUDA: If the knowledge serves treatment, then it's good, but only as a means to an end, not knowledge for the sake of knowledge. If a person comes to treatment and says, "I want for nothing, nothing hurts, I'm just curious about psychoanalysis," I send them home.

ESTHER: Okay. There's a measure of modesty in that, because the model doesn't claim to be true for everyone. It's a model that agrees to leave some people out . . . But hang on, in the second version, in which life starts from the Symbolic order, the Symbolic limits the person, which means the Symbolic is responsible for the deterministic aspect of life. In the first version – being born into the Real – we are born into chaos, which we organized through the other orders, so glad we had words with which to put order in the initial chaos. But in the second version, we are born into a family that has already decided what we'll be called and who we'll be. It's all over, and we have nowhere to run.

YEHUDA: And then trauma can save us, or meditation, or analysis. It's a way out of certainty, out of the certainty into which we were born.

ESTHER: You unravel it through analysis or meditation, and without even wanting to, out of a traumatic experience. But I learned from you, in different contexts, about the problematic nature of existing within one meaning. You've said that psychotics refuse to acknowledge the unconscious, because they grow to feel persecuted by it. Meaning, the unconscious is the father of ambivalence, the father of ambiguity. Right? You said psychotic people are afraid of ambiguity. Now you're saying that, actually, everyone is afraid of it.

YEHUDA: Psychotic people can't handle ambiguity, while neurotics can reject it or hold onto it. An obsessive person, for instance, holds onto the signifier, believing that they are what they think, but feel trapped, so they defy the signifier, refusing to be defined by it.

ESTHER: Because signifiers stifle them.

YEHUDA: Yes. So, if they're debating between studying law or computers, they think, "The profession I choose defines me." They identify completely with their signifier, and that's why the choice is so fateful. On the other hand, they refuse to be trampled by signifiers. Since they both love and hate the signifier, they remain ambivalent. What would we want to have happened in treatment? We want the person to realize these are just signifiers, and they never completely define them. In order not to be stifled by them, what they need is to give up their one-dimensionality. The same thing can happen with the experience of hysteria in a relationship. I want to be loved, but when someone loves me, I become an object, and that makes me miserable. So wait, do I want to be loved, or not? Can't live with it and can't live without it, that's the dynamic the obsessive has with the signifier and the hysterical with the desires of the other. Do you want to be defined or not?

ESTHER: Yes.

YEHUDA: The cure for the obsessive is to agree to be undefined. Definition can be used for specific purposes, such as entry to different groups, but not for the sole purpose of being defined. The hysterical need to be assured that they aren't wholly and completely loved. Parts of them are loved, but not all of them. We could sum this up by saying that the three orders are interrelated, and that their shared existence is called "reality." We could tell all sorts of linear tales about the way they are intertwined and switch between routes. We could discuss imbalance – when one or two of the orders are too dominant. If we translate this into ethical questions of the right way to live, the right way to live is in a way that provides room for each order; that allows us to face the senseless, the Real, without forcing a fantasy on reality, but also without being continually exposed to the distress of nonsense. Then we can use the persona of an imaginary self-image without confusing the identity of the subject with the identity of the ego. Meaning: we believe in language and in culture in a way that allows us to fit into them without sanctifying them.

Chapter 10

A Hike on the Mountain

This chapter will describe Esther's experience: of hiking on a mountain with other people, which brought up some questions about the human ability to hike on mountains. Yehuda and Esther will discuss the first and foremost reason for chatting on a mountain: fear of the Real, and speech as a safety net against it. This chapter will also discuss marriage wishes as insistence on Imaginary wholeness, art, and Zen Buddhism.

ESTHER: Our last two conversations dealt with the model of the three orders: Real, Imaginary, and Symbolic, and the Borromean knot that connects them. One interesting thing that came up is that the Symbolic acts as a mediator between the Imaginary and the Real, because the Imaginary aims to be a static, highly-aesthetic perfection, the Real is chaotic and unbearable in its chaotic nature, while the Symbolic is dynamic. We called it dynamic because it enables movement – not chaotic movement, not movement every which way, but organized yet flexible movement. Striving for order is a human quality, and the Symbolic order allows movement and space.

YEHUDA: I'll say it in a different way: this is how the Symbolic mediates. Each of them mediates in its own way. This is a certain reading of the Borromean knot, a possible view of the connection between the three orders.

ESTHER: Meaning, your starting point could also be a different corner of this triangle.

YEHUDA: Yes.

ESTHER: As central and as mediating the two others.

YEHUDA: Yes.

ESTHER: I'd like to remind both of us that this book is about ethics. Meaning that for each theory – including this three-order theory – we are behooved to formulate ethical ramifications. You discussed the mirror phase, and you said there's a point when the child hears somebody explain that they – the child – are the mirror image, which allows them to see themselves as a whole. You also said that contact with the Real is enabled through trauma. But it isn't clear what the story is for each order. Let me explain what I mean by way of

DOI: 10.4324/9781003342458-10

example: When we discussed giving up the Real, we talked about making do with the word rather than the thing itself. That was a glimpse into the function of language in human life – the Symbolic order.

YEHUDA: That's right.

ESTHER: Once we have a stronger foundation, we'll be able to discuss this triangle in contexts such as trauma and explain what happens there, or in the context of aging, which is a real process people are forced to encounter and experience emotionally, and then we can address the question of how a person can adjust to growing old or live – in the full sense of the word – with illness. That's ethics. I'm mentioning a few different cases in which the Real delivers a blow, and I'm interested in how the orders can be described in these cases and how it can work in a way that produces happiness.

A patient of mine experienced trauma: his business was foreclosed. He has PTSD and he came in for treatment. Six months after it happened, he is restless. The business was part of his identity. He says, "There are two things, actually, rather than one: there's what happened there – standing in my office and watching people shutting it down and not being able to do anything about it. And the other thing is its meaning – that a critical part of my life and my identity is ruined." Those are two different things. What happened in his mind as he watched these strangers walking into the thing, he created with his own two hands and packing it up? What happened? Why is it so impossible to accept? What does that question even mean? Paradoxically, one cannot accept it because of the Symbolic order, if I understand the definition correctly.

YEHUDA: It cannot be accepted in the Symbolic order.

ESTHER: What does "not accepting it" mean?

YEHUDA: It means it isn't written in the dictionary. Firefighters have it in their dictionary. First responders, who come to the sight of an accident or a terror attack and collect blown-up limbs, have it in their dictionary. It's called "findings," it's called "work," they've got a Symbolic order that allows them to accept this thing, to handle it, to protect themselves from it. But your patient never had to enter the event of his business being foreclosed into his dictionary. It has no place in his story, so now he has to change his story in order to fit it in.

ESTHER: But in order to not be able to accept it, he needs a story, and that's why I said the Symbolic is the reason the Real cannot be accepted.

YEHUDA: That's true. That's why the Real isn't exactly a pre-Symbolic state, and that's why, even as I created this path that starts with the Real, continues into the Imaginary (the mirror phase), and then coalesces the experience through the Symbolic, I emphasized that it was just one way to tell the story. It's the Real as a meaning existing in the triangular context, in the structure of interaction between the orders. The Real is traumatic not because the Symbolic doesn't exist, as in "pre-Symbolic" states, but because there is a Symbolic in which the Real is not contained. There is a Symbolic order in which the foreclosure of your patient's business is not contained, and is therefore traumatic. He has no words with which to experience the event, and it therefore remains outside of experience, raw.

ESTHER: "Outside of experience?"

YEHUDA: Yes. The Real is knocking at the door and that's the noise of the trauma, because it can't enter the Symbolic. If he writes a story about it, he can let it in through the writing. That's why treating the trauma, treating the encounter with the Real, would mean suturing the holes in the Symbolic with the help of a story. I had a patient who suffered of post-trauma following the Yom Kippur War. His way of stitching back the holes left by the image of the burnt tank was to talk about what happened there – in the tank, in the platoon, in the battalion, in the military, in reserve duty, and even in the geopolitical dynamic between Israel, the United States, and Egypt, no less. He required an entire encyclopedia just to define a single word.

ESTHER: A single word?

YEHUDA: He needed this whole enormous story to give meaning to one word – trauma. To overcome trauma through a word, when the context needed for the word is the entire world; the entire geopolitical history of the war.

ESTHER: And yet there is something knocking on the doors of consciousness that cannot come in.

YEHUDA: Right. There is something that will never be accepted.

ESTHER: But there's no need to experience trauma for this purpose, because in reality we are always living in the Real –

YEHUDA: Right.

ESTHER: Living in the Real but denying the Real?

YEHUDA: One could take, for example, an obsessive symptom –

ESTHER: Because the obsessive knows; they see the frivolity of it all, all the time.

YEHUDA: Exactly.

ESTHER: Meaning, in a way, they see the Real.

YEHUDA: Right, but they also don't give up: they demand that meaning be there and won't accept the rift between the Real and meaning.

ESTHER: Yes. They are upset at meaning for not being able to contain the Real.

YEHUDA: Right.

ESTHER: For being nothing but a delusion.

YEHUDA: Exactly. That's exactly right. On the one hand, they are sober enough to see it's a delusion. On the other hand, they protest against it because they demand complete congruence between the word and the thing, and it doesn't work, so they try again and again, hoping it would work this time. But they are also honest with themselves, admitting it never works, unlike those who delude themselves that the word is the thing.

ESTHER: Hysteria, for instance. No?

YEHUDA: Not necessarily.

ESTHER: Why not? Say something about hysteria in this context, characterize it in the context of the orders.

YEHUDA: The way the hysteric protests the delusion of symbolism is its attribution to a master –

ESTHER: Oh! So they've been duped.

YEHUDA: They cast blame on a person. They attribute what they've experienced as fraud to some kind of master –

ESTHER: Who didn't keep their promise.

YEHUDA: And then the hysteric person makes it their goal to bring down the master, to prove to the mater that they don't control things. Meaning, to prove that the Symbolic doesn't contain the Real, to uncover the fakery. But since they aren't happy with this result either, they lift the master back onto their throne. So the difference is that the one in charge of the symbolic stability that continues to be undermined is an image of some kind of leader, someone who claims –

ESTHER: To arrange the world, but they don't.

YEHUDA: That's right.

ESTHER: They don't arrange the world; they leave flaws that hurt us.

YEHUDA: Right. That's why the hysterical person dedicates their life to proving the master's flaw. A flaw that they don't want to admit is inevitable, that that's what life is like; imperfect. The hysterical complaining enforces the assumption that things could be different.

ESTHER: In that case, you are saying that believing in God is a hysterical symptom.

YEHUDA: If it's a God we blame, pointing to His flaws and being disappointed by God's concerns about truth and justice, then yes. There's an ethical answer here: the goal is to acknowledge the partiality of the Symbolic and the Imaginary in terms of their ability to contain the Real. Meaning, it's best to know that words aren't things, and therefore we don't need to prove they aren't. We can release ourselves of the need to prove the failure of the order, because its failure is preordained. Now let's move on to something more interesting.

ESTHER: Let's use this gap between the Symbolic and the Real. There's always a gap, and that is the most interesting loophole in reality.

YEHUDA: That's why art is making up something senseless, so that this gap can cause the audience to speak in an attempt to fill it, to create meaning. That means that an artist doesn't create meanings, but stimulates people to create them.

ESTHER: So, you're saying that there is no place for the Real in consciousness, so it's sort of closer to the body?

YEHUDA: Closer to the body, closer to *jouissance* and when it's connected to language it's to single words that don't connect to other words to form meaning

ESTHER: That's what I don't understand.

YEHUDA: Those are the unbearable things, whether it's old age or death or –

ESTHER: Sex?

YEHUDA: Sure, yes. We don't learn sex, we learn encyclopedias. You can't teach sex with words; it doesn't fit into words you can pass on.

ESTHER: Same goes for giving birth.

YEHUDA: Okay.

ESTHER: And pregnancy.

YEHUDA: Okay.

ESTHER: Right?

YEHUDA: Yes. I'd say everything has an aspect that doesn't fit in its word.

ESTHER: You'd say that about every single thing!

YEHUDA: Yes. The word doesn't cover all aspects of what it's meant to represent.

ESTHER: The experience it's meant to represent.

YEHUDA: That's right.

ESTHER: Because you want to stay in epistemology – not the "thing," right? The experience.

YEHUDA: But that's also the thing in itself. There's this thing (knocks on the table) and yet, calling it "table" is missing something.

ESTHER: Yes.

YEHUDA: The thing is missed.

ESTHER: All the time.

YEHUDA: That is the uncontainable Real. So let's be more precise: this is a coffee table. But that isn't accurate either. It'll always be inaccurate.

ESTHER: Yes, why does it create such a problem?

YEHUDA: It doesn't have to. We could live in peace with the fact that the map cannot cover the terrain. This process, of learning to make peace with the limitations of the Symbolic is a transition from impotence to helplessness.

ESTHER: Got it. But I'd like to turn your attention to something else: I'm saying there's a difficulty to live with the Real rather than a difficulty to live with the partiality of the Symbolic. It's something else.

YEHUDA: Okay.

ESTHER: For example, let's think of people going on a hike. It's a Saturday, they pack a bag and are ready to walk their asses off at age fifty and climb up some mountains. So they're hiking through the mountains. They go on hiking through the mountains but they aren't really there, because they're talking the whole time, hiking through the mountains and talking rather than hiking through the mountains full stop. Zen Buddhism instructs you differently – if you're on the mountain, be on the mountain. Why do you keep escaping from the mountain? You came here especially to see it, to be here. It's gorgeous, look! Instead, they talk. That's what I'm talking about. It's a resistance to the Real, no less. And even when it comes to beauty, you realize you don't really have anything to say about it. You can't really talk about it. You can tell the other person, oh, how pretty, but that's more or less where it ends. And then why do you have to blab about everything that's going on at your kid's school while you're hiking through the mountains? It's this kind of talk that makes me choose to hike alone . . .

YEHUDA: Alone?

ESTHER: Sure.

YEHUDA: Alone is what we're escaping from.

ESTHER: Now explain why.

YEHUDA: *Jouissance* of the Real is alone.

ESTHER: What does that mean?

YEHUDA: Like in masturbation. Alone.

ESTHER: It's more real, but it isn't more *jouissance*.

YEHUDA: There is no communication. The thing that connects people is the Symbolic matrix; the fact that they both function in a system that connects them.

ESTHER: So does one have to hold on to the Symbolic? Does one have to speak to one's walking partner out of a duty to hold onto the Symbolic?

YEHUDA: Exactly. The Symbolic keeps the subjects bound to each other through their representing signifiers. I am represented by my name, you are represented by your name, our names are connected, we are connected through our names, our shared vocabulary. As soon as it's just us and the mountains, moved by its beauty without any space for talking, there is no communication, no togetherness. It's enough for you to think that you wish you could communicate the awe you sense on the mountain to your friend, and realize that words are not enough, to stop being alone. The words don't have to be expressed, as in reading or writing, or thinking.

ESTHER: Oy-oy-oy. Let's talk for a bit about this oy-oy-oy of no togetherness.

YEHUDA: We could say something here about the preferable way to live. Preferably, one's experience isn't limited only to what can be communicated.

ESTHER: Very preferably. So can we talk about this for a moment? Because you see I come off as a freak because of my choice to live alone. A friend read one of my books and said exactly what I wanted her to: she said it was a good book and that the language was wonderful. Meaning, she was able to skip over the "Real" in the book and see the beauty of it. That was my wish, the very opposite of my fear – that no one would see the beauty in the book. It made me so happy. And then, after she finished praising the book, she said, "But I can't help myself; I still wish for you to find love, to find a romantic relationship." The truth is, it was touching. But come to think of it, it wasn't that she was wishing me some kind of unique pleasure she herself had experienced. It was more like she had to – *had to!* – wish that for me. Now, you know that irks me because it puts me in a position of supposed lack, a very intense lack, and specifically the kind of lack that is connected in normative thought with being problematic. It's a lack that has a certain social-ethical hierarchy. It isn't a lack like any other. It signals a basic failure, and it creates –

YEHUDA: A status.

ESTHER: Precisely.

YEHUDA: Yes.

ESTHER: And she just wanted me to have that status, that Imaginary societal concept.

YEHUDA: Yes.

ESTHER: If I answered her honestly, I would have said, "Take a look at your own life and tell me what I'm missing out on. What am I actually missing?" But she *had to*, had to offer it to – no, not offer. *Wish* it for me – in order to keep me in the picture. Then you see our attitude toward loneliness and toward those who welcome it. First of all, we don't believe them, so much so that even I have trouble believing myself. It's a kind of big Other anxiety, as if there is an imperative to strive – or, as psychologists call it, to yearn – for a romantic relationship, just as there is an imperative to chat when hiking in a group. One must live together, or at least to strive to. Up until now, I interpreted this through evolutionary survival concepts – the survival of the race demands that we be two rather than one, something like that. But beyond that, you can recognize a panicked puzzlement: "She isn't married . . ." What's wrong with you people? Now, let's not make a joke out of it but really take a look, even though to me it really does seem like a pure, normative joke.

YEHUDA: I think the question "married or unmarried" has to do with the question of participation in the Symbolic. On the other hand, writing the book is also a participation in the Symbolic.

ESTHER: Yes, that's my solution, exactly.

YEHUDA: There is no difference in terms of us being subjects embedded in humanity through language: you can be married; you can be a writer – as long as you are included in language.

ESTHER: Of course, of course. You'll find your way, there are countless ways. That's great.

YEHUDA: And while we have the Imaginary enter the fray through status differences between the whole and the flawed –

ESTHER: Oh, the "whole . . ."

YEHUDA: Wait a minute. Since we are all within language, all flawed, all experiencing the partiality of language, there is a solidarity in this –

ESTHER: But they don't see it. They define wholeness through couples, like Noah's Ark, the kind of place where being on one's own is uncomfortable because it's a disruption of the order. My friend wasn't willing to accept the camaraderie of the lacking! She enjoyed the book immensely, but then she had to turn it around, as if there is a lack that would be too dangerous not to point out . . .

YEHUDA: But the new element here is the Imaginary. On the one hand, you're a great writer, the revered mirror image. But on the other hand, she's married and you aren't, so it turns around.

ESTHER: But wait, that's very specific. I don't want to talk about envy. Let's go back to where we were before –

YEHUDA: But wait, there's an imaginary connection here, because the Imaginary belief is that if only you were married, you'd want for nothing.

ESTHER: Right.

YEHUDA: The Imaginary strives for wholeness.

ESTHER: Yes, yes, that's it. Yes, I'm great, but I'm just missing this one thing and she wishes I get it. She insisted it was love . . .

YEHUDA: Yes, Yes.

ESTHER: So okay, you took this in a different direction.

YEHUDA: While beauty is about what you do with the lack!

ESTHER: Right.

YEHUDA: Beauty is determined in relationship to lack.

ESTHER: In the absence.

YEHUDA: Beauty does something to lack.

ESTHER: It beautifies it.

YEHUDA: Yes.

ESTHER: Does it call it by a name? What does it do to it? And how?

YEHUDA: It gives it proportions, like the composition of a painting, like depth perspective, like removing material to create a sculpture. The aesthetics is the relationship between what is and what isn't. It gives space to what isn't, but while relating to what is. Like the Golden Ratio, which is attributed to Pythagoras's students.

ESTHER: Yes.

YEHUDA: But it isn't like the aesthetics fill the void.

ESTHER: Not at all.

YEHUDA: It gives shape to the lack. That's why your friend contradicted herself about your book: "How lovely, you're giving shape to the lack. Now let's fill it up!"

ESTHER: Yes. But this was a different interpretation. We are saying the problem is the lack and the question is how to interpret or deal with the lack. This is how we solved the problem of my friend's reaction. Now let's go back to the mountain, where people are hiking and chatting. That's the word – chatting. Chatting frivolously, preferring their prattle to the possibility of truly being on the mountain. What's with this anxiety? That's what I want to know. To me, it's the same as wishing me love or a relationship or whatever. Let's talk about that.

YEHUDA: I'm not sure why we ought to judge it.

ESTHER: Why we ought to judge it?

YEHUDA: There's judgment here.

ESTHER: Certainly. Because I think it's ignorant.

YEHUDA: People like to chat.

ESTHER: No, no, no, Yehuda, no, no, they can't help themselves. Forget love it, they can't *not* chat. This is a limitation, without a doubt.

YEHUDA: I'm not sure it is.

ESTHER: It's definitely a limitation. It's like – don't you see? – it's like you're walking there and a bird tweets. Wait, let me bring you into it, how can you not understand?

YEHUDA: Wait, I'm telling you I can address this if I speak to the chatting person themselves and they tell me that no one wanted to chat with them and they felt anxious.

ESTHER: Of course, they'll say that.

YEHUDA: If they say that then I'd treat them and figure out where the anxiety comes from.

ESTHER: You said it before – it comes from being left alone.

YEHUDA: Okay.

ESTHER: What's the point? Why is it so scary?

YEHUDA: It's scary by definition. It's threatening. It's the Real. You ask why the threatening is threatening? By being threatening we realize it's Real.

ESTHER: It's a reverse course, a path from effect to cause, which is fine, but that's just a possibility.

YEHUDA: Be more specific, maybe we aren't understanding each other.

ESTHER: Yeah, it's odd that you're not understanding this. So odd.

YEHUDA: It's not that I don't understand, I'm just reluctant to take on a condescending imagining perspective about it, so I need the person to tell me what hurts them.

ESTHER: I'm really talking to you about what Buddhism refers to as suffering. This is the suffering referred to in Buddhism. And this suffering is caused, for instance, by our preference for fixed things instead of endless dynamism.

YEHUDA: That's it! That's neurosis. We all share a public delusion called language. No, I'm sorry, not language – social institutions.

ESTHER: Culture. Civilization.

YEHUDA: Yes. The purpose of analysis is to shake off neurosis. Meaning, to shake off our grip of the sense, which is Imaginary-Symbolic, and thus be able to hike through the mountain without having to reduce the experience only to what can be communicated.

ESTHER: Meaning, to let go of the Symbolic in order to allow other elements of existence –

YEHUDA: The gap between a child and their mother is the gap between the word and the thing. Freudian castration, perpetrated by a father who sets limits for the child and pushes them away from the mother, isn't something personal that could be corrected if only one had different parents. That's why the neurotic patient spends the first half of treatment complaining about their parents. Later on, they acknowledge the fact that the problem is structural, like the Borromean knot – that these three orders exist, and that the Symbolic is only one of them. It doesn't contain everything. Therefore, to bring it back to Zen Buddhism, the chatting person doesn't want to face the "no-words."

ESTHER: That's right.

YEHUDA: Because they have this fantasy –

ESTHER: That there are words for everything.

YEHUDA: That this gap can be filled. It's like thinking, "If I only had different parents, everything would be perfect. I would lack nothing."

ESTHER: All right.

YEHUDA: They won't give up objects, either. They won't remain only with thing that cannot be known. From the obsessive aspect, they have to know everything. They won't stand having people who don't like them, just like hysterics. But what can you do? Different strokes for different folks . . .

ESTHER: Okay. So, you mean that chatting on the mountain is a battle against lack.

YEHUDA: Yes.

ESTHER: Ultimately, it's the choice.

YEHUDA: Yes.

ESTHER: To describe it that way.

YEHUDA: Yes.

ESTHER: So that's the thing, and that's why I feel the way I do. I feel like there's a kind of public deception I can't be a part of.

YEHUDA: You're looking for partners who can be silent on the mountain together, with whom you can share the lack and be together – together in the sense that we both are familiar with the experience of a definition that never quite lives up to its promise.

ESTHER: Exactly.

YEHUDA: That togetherness is called love.

ESTHER: Okay.

YEHUDA: Love, unlike symbiosis, which is not a Lacanian word, but describes the fantasy of a love that lacks for nothing. Love means living in peace with the lack of symbiosis, with the lack of perfection in the relationship, with the lack of satisfaction. To use Lacan's words –

ESTHER: Great, yes.

YEHUDA: Love is the answer to the lack of a sexual relationship.

ESTHER: Yes.

YEHUDA: A sexual relationship is a scenario where things complete each other fully.

ESTHER: Yes.

YEHUDA: Love is being together in the absence of a sexual relationship.

ESTHER: All right, okay, I sort of get it now. It references Zen. In Zen one is taught not to even try to wrap the tangible with words. Now, as soon as I say "taught," I'm already presenting a paradox. There's a saying in Buddhist training: "Don't-know mind." The unknowing mind. One must learn to give up the possibility of knowing, okay? And not for the sake of ignorance or reduction, but for the sake of ability. For the sake of expanding our ability to carry it without knowing it. You don't always have to pack everything so tight that it fits under the symbolic rug. One has to stop trying to shrink her experience, and finally herself, to the size of the Symbolic, of culture, of language, and then find out by experience that is might look scary, but it isn't really. On the contrary. You realize you'll crash into reality anyway, like it or not. So open your mind, expand your horizons – no, don't expand them, open them up completely – and see what it's like. Okay?

YEHUDA: People can recognize this release in nonsense humor. "Knock, knock!" "Who's there?" "Orange!" "Orange who?" "Orange you glad I didn't say banana?" If we were in the Symbolic order we'd expect a satisfying response, but we'll never be fully satisfied about who's knocking at the door. We'll never know. What we receive as substitute is a joke at the expense of language.

ESTHER: Yes.

YEHUDA: You want a literal response? Here you go. Now see how unsatisfying it is. Joke's over and you'll never get a satisfying answer.

ESTHER: Yes.

YEHUDA: And we laugh because we are exempt from chasing sense. We're free – for a moment! – of the edict to find the sense in things.

ESTHER: Let's stop. Let's stop right here.

Chapter 11

On Anxiety

The first part of this chapter will deal with anxiety, which is one of the most common complaints of modern humanity (along with depression, which will be discussed in the next chapter); about Freud's theory of anxiety (the suppression of undesirable drives); about Lacan's theory of anxiety (and his special addition of anxiety of the nameless); and about the connection between anxiety and identity.

The second part of the chapter will discuss the relationship between anxiety and sexuality: What differentiates women from men?

And finally, the connection between anxiety and faith.

Part 1: Anxiety in Freud and Lacan

YEHUDA: Today we're going to talk about anxiety.

ESTHER: Fantastic. Let's start with a question: What is it? Anxiety has become such an overused word. I think it's a cultural phenomenon. Complaints about depression and anxiety are all around us. Patients come in with self-reported anxiety, and sometimes I feel that this word is covering other issues. A person says "I'm anxious," labeling themselves without undertaking the question of why they are anxious. This leads to a range of behaviors and functions, when in fact, it isn't about anxiety, but about conflict.

YEHUDA: People do indeed use the word anxiety to refer to other things or to avoid naming things. I think that's the essence of anxiety.

ESTHER: That's the essence? Avoiding naming things?

YEHUDA: Precisely. So, since you've asked what anxiety is, let's start with the attempt to avoid naming things. That's anxiety in the Freudian sense, anxiety of the repressed thing. We will continue with the possibility that things actually have no name – that is the Lacanian anxiety, the anxiety of the unnamable. It is unnamable not because we have repressed its name, but because it has no name. A person has an experience but is unable to name it. They feel pain but cannot get a diagnosis. They develop hypochondria. Hypochondria in that case may be seen as an attempt to name an anxiety in order to reduce

DOI: 10.4324/9781003342458-11

it. There are two basic possibilities: either the person cannot name the experience, and it is therefore anxiety; or the person attempts not to name it, and it therefore stays in the amorphic form of anxiety. In both cases, anxiety is a thing without a name, a definition, or a word.

ESTHER: When you speak of this unnamable thing, are you saying it, in essence, has no name? Or are you saying the patient hasn't found the name?

YEHUDA: That depends on whether you subscribe to Freud or Lacan. According to Lacan, it can be a "Freudian" anxiety – an anxiety of something named and repressed – or (and this is Lacan's innovation), an anxiety of the unnamable.

ESTHER: The first type of anxiety is the anxiety of the person who doesn't want to know.

YEHUDA: Yes. But as we've already learned, language can't contain everything. The map can't cover every terrain, and words can't name the entire world. Something always remains beyond what can be seen – the Imaginary – and beyond what can be formulated – the Symbolic. There's something that cannot enter. I'd call it a life energy, a libido that cannot cling to a specific fetish, that cannot achieve cathexis, that cannot bind. It remains free-floating, outside of the Imaginary or the Symbolic.

ESTHER: But if what you're talking about is a life force, why does it turn into anxiety?

YEHUDA: Because the alternative is turning into depression.

ESTHER: Why? It's a life force that cannot find its expression.

YEHUDA: That's right. It cannot find it's expression, or it has no expression.

ESTHER: But it's alive! It's lively. Why would it become anxiety? Why doesn't it transform instead into exercise?

YEHUDA: Exercise is a name.

ESTHER: Right; so it finds its expression . . .

YEHUDA: Exactly. It's desire that is not articulated. If we can speak it, we structure it in language, whether through learning or invention, we are able to act. We have a path.

ESTHER: So, this is a vitality that cannot find its expression, and its fate is to transform into anxiety.

YEHUDA: Yes.

ESTHER: I don't understand the causality.

YEHUDA: There are two causes: one is the Freudian cause. Freud was a positivist, so he did not consider the unnamable. The oceanic experience, or female *jouissance*, was foreign to him. It was the thing beyond a name. He never really completed *Beyond the Pleasure Principle*, where he tried to treat trauma. He didn't solve the enigma of trauma. So, the Freudian anxiety is something that has a name we've repressed. We've hidden it away in a locked drawer and are afraid to think about it because we're ashamed of our own drives. If anyone names them for us, we feel anxiety and repulsion and want to get away. That's one form of anxiety, which stems from the desire not to know about the drive. Another form is the anxiety of fulfilling the drive; a fear of temptation that might lead to fulfilling the drive. That's still Freudian, because according to Freud the drive is knowable. Lacan, on the other hand, argues that not all sexual energy is formulated into drives, fetishes, programs, wishes, ambitions. Not all of this energy can be channeled or packaged in words, arranged into stories. So, this thing – the *jouissance* that remains outside of the Symbolic, the Imaginary, and outside of sense, which is Imaginary and Symbolic put together – is the Real. Anxiety is fear of the Real. What happens when one cannot protect oneself from it? Trauma. That's why post-trauma is anxiety.

ESTHER: You said that anxiety of the unnamable is fear of the Real only at the very end of your explanation. Why didn't you open with that?

YEHUDA: Because that isn't the foundation. The foundation of anxiety is a threat against the subject. Just as fear is connected to organic survival, anxiety is connected to symbolic survival, meaning, an undermining of identity.

Let's call it "identity" in layman's terms. I'll say "identity" instead of "subject." I'm referring to a personal threat, but not against my physical body, but against my cultural, Symbolic, Imaginary, or virtual existence. A danger to the solid existence of my identity. When can identity be undermined? If, in the first example, there's something I'm embarrassed to know about myself, then knowing that those certain drives exist within me undermines my identity, and that is the cause of anxiety. If our culture accepted these drives, they wouldn't threaten our identity.

ESTHER: All right. Does the aging example fit the bill? A beautiful woman growing old?

YEHUDA: That depends. It isn't a fear of knowing about drives but another form of threat to the subject. Yes, it can create anxiety. The more identified she feels with the previous image of herself, which is no longer relevant, the less like herself she feels. Like the man you mentioned who lost his identity when he went bankrupt. In that sense, the number of anxieties is the same as the number of threats to the subject.

ESTHER: And what about illness? Is that a threat to the subject?

YEHUDA: It depends on how much your self-definition revolves around health. Take note: those who have illness as the basis of their self-definition will experience an anxiety of recovery.

All forms of anxiety stem from a threat to self-definition. That's why a discussion of the broad term "anxiety" is a discussion of the threat to self-definition. There are different forms of self-definition. One is: I'm a common person, polite, more or less normative. In that case, any repressed drive that is considered indecorous threatens self-definition. It will also threaten self-definition if it comes true. Anything undefined would also certainly threaten self-definition by virtue of not being defined. Other forms of anxiety – let's call them symbiosis or excessive proximity – stem from the fact that a lack of clear boundaries between myself and another blurs my self-definition. We must remember that a definition is a kind of border between an individual and their surroundings, and has a function of preserving the sense of individuality.

ESTHER: The subjectivity.

YEHUDA: The distinct individual, the ego, is an avatar of the subject, and the threat to it creates anxiety. Those who don't identify themselves with their egos as much will experience less anxiety of a threat to their individuality. That's why one of the forms of anxiety is believing someone wants something from me that I cannot define; people are staring and I don't know why. It's anxiety-inducing because my wishes and the wishes of another mix together. My self-definition as a subject is founded on my will: I have a will and I am the wanter. If 'we' have a will, then it isn't me who is the wanter anymore. Wills mixing together can create anxiety.

ESTHER: That's what I wanted to ask you about. When someone says, "I don't know if I'm the one who wants to study medicine or if my parents want me to," they are correct.

YEHUDA: Yes.

ESTHER: Let me explain my argument. Each person's growth as a subject is connected – in various ways – to their parents' wishes; wishes their parents imparted to them, often without being aware of it. They identify with their parents, internalizing their wishes. In this sense, the question of whether I am the one who wants to be a doctor or if this wish has been "implanted" into me is valid and yet unanswerable.

YEHUDA: Indeed! A child whose parents' wishes were never imposed on them is unfortunate. They have no wishes.

ESTHER: On the one hand, there is the cultural fantasy, the kind of "new right" – wishing nothing for your child other than that they "be happy."

YEHUDA: That is the narcissistic fantasy of the self-made person, free of any outside influence.

ESTHER: In that case, when someone tells me – often in complaint – "I don't know if I want that or if someone else wants it for me" – then we at the clinic must work to make sure they are convinced it is their own wish they are following.

YEHUDA: Correct.

ESTHER: But, in truth, it's an illusion. The term "my wish" is unrealistic, because a subject's wishes are never fully their own.

YEHUDA: No, "my wish" is not an illusion. My approach to it is, "It's true that you want it and it's true that your parents wanted you to want it. It's true that these wishes are mixed up. What we should care about is not whether this is your refined, self-invented, sterile wish; what we should care about is whether you intend to act on this wish. Only you can decide whether or not to actually study medicine."

ESTHER: Whether or not you choose to study medicine.

YEHUDA: That's why I would say that every wish within you is a wish your parents planted in you. Some of them are reversed – meaning you want the opposite of what they want, or actively don't want the thing they want, because you're rebelling against their wishes. But even a reversal of parental wishes is nothing more than your refusal to obey their wishes. In fact, all you need to do is choose which of their wishes to adopt. As soon as you've adopted them, they are your own.

ESTHER: Okay.

YEHUDA: Now: some of your parents' wishes you've already adopted unconsciously, and you're feeling the desire to fulfil them. That only confirms the fact that they've been adopted. You might still be debating about another part of their wishes. Growing up is the ability to do what you want even though other people also want it from you.

The lack of clarity regarding the question of whether you want it or not creates anxiety. Distilling the wishes – supposedly filtering out others' wishes – is not what leads to owning the wish. This kind of distillation empties the subject of wishes, since the subject is necessarily intertwined with others. As soon as I've made a decision, the wish becomes my own. Now I know what I want, and my anxiety lessens. One can think of agoraphobia as a defense against the kind of anxiety we're discussing right now: a person doesn't want to go outside lest they interact with others and be invaded by their wishes, which would cause anxiety. The unconscious meaning of agoraphobia is anxiety of excessive physical proximity to other people. It's a stifling caused by a lack of barrier between the subject and others, as if refusing the desire of the other as part of the desire of the subject can keep a barrier between subject and other.

ESTHER: But what is this barrier? It doesn't truly exist.

YEHUDA: It allows a sense of individuality, self-identity.

ESTHER: Yes, but what is the barrier? What is it made of?

YEHUDA: It's made of the ego. The ego carries the function of separateness.

ESTHER: But the ego is an illusion, and therefore separateness is an illusion.

YEHUDA: The question is, is the illusion maintained? Can I say, "Here are my boundaries."

ESTHER: It's an illusion.

YEHUDA: The Symbolic is an illusion too. The only order that isn't an illusion is the Real. Anxiety is fear of the dismantling of the illusion that maintains an identity.

ESTHER: So, let's assume a person is unable to maintain the experience of separateness, of being an individual subject. They cannot maintain it, cannot tell their wishes from others', and this generates anxiety.

YEHUDA: Yes. Anxiety of that kind – unlike the anxiety of energy that finds no object to hang onto – is more reminiscent of distress, the experience of excess, of a burden that must be shed.

ESTHER: Distressed by the wishes of another?

YEHUDA: Yes. And in this case one must undergo a process of separating from the other's wishes.

ESTHER: Is this "the other's desires?"

YEHUDA: Yes. Now let's take things one step further: it would be more accurate to talk about this as the other's *jouissance*. The other's desire is the question of "What should I do with my life? What is my role in this world?" while the other's *jouissance* is the situation in which I'm anxious in the paranoid sense: "Another is going to use me, objectify me, take away my subjectivity." If we take this one step further, the subject themselves are tempted to merge with another and be their object. It isn't coming only from the other. The subject longs to merge with the other.

ESTHER: I don't understand that.

YEHUDA: A longing for something orgiastic; for merging with another.

ESTHER: Like sex?

YEHUDA: The question is whether people look for it outside of sex.

ESTHER: Such as love poems?

YEHUDA: If it can be formulated in a poem the anxiety lessens.

ESTHER: Okay, so that's why we formulate it.

YEHUDA: There is an incestuous drive to merge with the other. The superficial form this drive takes is, "The parent wants to merge with me and I must defend myself."

ESTHER: It's projected and reversed.

YEHUDA: Right. Of course, it could truly exist, the fact of people wanting to merge with me, and that's threatening. But I have a part in this too; the subject has drives too – this death drive toward merging, regression, incestuous fantasy. And this is where we go back to Freud, because it is an anxiety about the desires of the subject themselves.

ESTHER: But it's a justified anxiety . . . You're running ahead today and I'm having trouble keeping up. You're using eighteen concepts in every sentence you say.

YEHUDA: You're right, you're right.

ESTHER: So here I am, trying to catch up: is this what you call the death drive? The desire to merge?

YEHUDA: Yes.

ESTHER: Why do you call it a death drive?

YEHUDA: Because existence is a kind of separateness. There is no existence in merging. You gave the example of sex. Self-awareness is erased in *jouissance*. There is self-oblivion in *jouissance*.

ESTHER: Okay, so there is no Symbolic existence.

YEHUDA: No existence at all.

ESTHER: There is Real existence.

YEHUDA: Then let me distinguish existence from being. There is existence in the Real sense, but no being, which is the symbolic aspect of existence. Lacan distinguishes "existence" from "being." The being is erased. "Existence" refers to the organic, to the question of whether a creature is alive or dead.

ESTHER: And "being" refers to a conscious, mental existence. Okay, I got you. Now, let me make an associative leap. I'm not sure it's relevant, but let me try. We spoke recently about the woman's *jouissance*. It seems related.

YEHUDA: It is. So let's start our next topic.

Part 2: Anxiety in Relation to Gender and Sexuality

YEHUDA: There is a category of phenomena which we can generally refer to as "the nullifying of the subject." The mythological form of this drive is the longing to return to the womb, to merge with the mother's body and become like one of her organs. Other forms are the Oedipal fantasy or regression to oral or anal states of returning the lost object. There is an anxiety of fulfilling the regressive fantasy, the general focus of which is turning into another's object.

ESTHER: This is the height of masochism. Is that what you mean?

YEHUDA: No; masochism is a solution. The masochist, as we've discussed in the chapter focused on the phenomenon, is a rejected object.

ESTHER: Yes.

YEHUDA: And by being rejected, they rescue themselves from being attached and indistinct. That's why it's a solution.

ESTHER: They found a way of being separate, that's why it's a solution.

YEHUDA: Indeed. The state of the attached, of the unseparated, evokes anxiety.

ESTHER: Yes. It evokes anxiety and paranoia.

YEHUDA: "Paranoia" refers to fear of something coming at me, about to take over me and merge with me. One type of paranoia is erotomania. That's even more transparent: "Everybody wants to have sex with me." That is the threatening form, and let us not be mistaken – this is not some kind of neurotic bragging, like, "I'm so attractive." It's a true experience of threat.

ESTHER: What does this have to do with a woman's *jouissance*?

YEHUDA: The female *jouissance* is a way of talking about a sexuality that breaks boundaries, that trespasses.

ESTHER: What is the boundary?

YEHUDA: The phallus creates a boundary. Masculine sexuality is represented by the phallus. You might say the masculine *jouissance* has a foundation and a ceiling. Meaning, there is an available fetish through which sexuality can be turned on, but it has a very defined end: the man ejaculates and it's over. A woman has less of an opening foundation. Her sexuality isn't as focused on a defined fetish, but the pleasure is greater.

ESTHER: How do you know it's greater? Why do you say it's greater? What does "greater" mean? Stronger?

YEHUDA: Yes. A woman can have multiple orgasms.

ESTHER: That's what you mean. Okay. So, her pleasure is less defined both in its beginning and in its end.

YEHUDA: Correct.

ESTHER: And then?

YEHUDA: The definability, that is an aspect of male sexuality. Indefinability is an aspect of female sexuality.

ESTHER: Yes, okay. So, there was a reason I associated female *jouissance* with an indefinability that generates anxiety.

YEHUDA: And there's more: phallic sexuality is more fixated on erogenous zones; on objects.

ESTHER: Yes, that's what I mean by "fetish."

YEHUDA: But female sexuality is harder to point to and define specifically.

ESTHER: All right. That connects to the things we just discussed, because here too, in the context of female *jouissance*, you are talking about something shapeless.

YEHUDA: It's possible then that Freud himself was anxious about female sexuality.

ESTHER: Some say so, yes. Especially women say so.

YEHUDA: Because this boundless thing –

ESTHER: Can certainly awake anxiety in a man.

YEHUDA: Yes.

ESTHER: And that leads to premature ejaculation, to try and put a quick end to it.

YEHUDA: Or helplessness. Yes.

ESTHER: Put an end to it – why? Can you explain the anxiety it generates in a man?

YEHUDA: The woman's pleasure seems to obliterate him, as if tempting him to become its object.

ESTHER: Is it like he forgets himself inside of her? Is that what you're saying?

YEHUDA: Yes, yes, yes.

ESTHER: He'll lose himself inside of her, forgetting himself.

YEHUDA: He'll lose himself.

ESTHER: Inside that infinity, inside that ocean.

YEHUDA: Exactly so.

ESTHER: The Real.

YEHUDA: Yes.

ESTHER: We're back to the Real.

YEHUDA: Female sexuality is another name for the Real.

ESTHER: I get it. To an extent.

YEHUDA: The psychotic experience and the mystic experience are other names for the Real. Trauma is another one, too. What is the difference between all of these names? That in each one we do something else.

ESTHER: Yes. Yes. My association (with female *jouissance*), it turns out, is justified. It has to do with this nameless or limitless thing that has no clear or inherent beginning or end. And then whoever faces it can become anxious. Is this a way for us to formulate things in a sexual context, just as we'd discussed a man-facing female *jouissance*?

YEHUDA: Yes.

ESTHER: Yes, but it also creates anxiety in the woman herself.

YEHUDA: About this *Jouissance.*

ESTHER: Yes.

YEHUDA: Of course. It resembles hypochondria: there are sensations, experiences, happenings related to the body, related to pleasure, which cannot be named.

ESTHER: No.

YEHUDA: Think about a woman submerged in her own *jouissance* in a manner inspiring anxiety. Then she asks herself if she has a medical problem and starts to find a solution.

ESTHER: Yes.

YEHUDA: Because putting it in a medical context is a way of naming it. But it isn't a medical problem, so the diagnosis doesn't help, and so she goes off looking for another. This chase after a lost diagnosis – that's hypochondria. Just realize, it can all start from a frightening sexual arousal.

ESTHER: Wait, wait, wait. First of all, I'm still back there with that frightened woman. A woman is sitting here, thinking about this anxiety we're discussing. I myself can't find a name for it. Maybe I failed to understand the process you described.

YEHUDA: Then let me start from a different direction. I think it also has to do with anatomical difference.

ESTHER: How so?

YEHUDA: A lizard can be anxious about being eaten and detach its tail from its body so that only the tail is eaten. That way, it can run away.

ESTHER: Yes.

YEHUDA: The tail is the phallus. The tail is the thing about which a person can say, "Someone wants something from me" rather than "Someone wants all of me."

ESTHER: Okay.

YEHUDA: A man has an easier time saying "someone wants something from me" without panicking. A woman more easily starts to think, "someone wants all of me."

ESTHER: Yes. And that creates anxiety. The name of the anxiety is: I'm being objectified.

YEHUDA: Precisely.

ESTHER: That's where the story begins! There it is, that feminist claim of being objectified.

YEHUDA: Right. The woman is the object, and the object is wanted, is used, is taken pleasure in, etc. The man has the option of saying, "*I'm* not an object; I *have* an object." This is also the source of the analogy between a phallus and a woman: both of them are something about which a man can say: "I have an object." It can be "I have a big penis" or "I have a beautiful woman." In that sense, they are analogues, the phallus and the woman.

ESTHER: Because a man can do that. That's his solution, his way of avoiding becoming an object and losing himself.

YEHUDA: His solution is being able to detach his tail and free himself from the anxiety that someone wants all of him.

ESTHER: Of being drowned in somebody else's desire.

YEHUDA: That's right. Castration is a solution for anxiety.

ESTHER: Okay.

YEHUDA: A woman doesn't have that castration option. There's nothing to castrate.

ESTHER: Because she is everything, because all of her is wanted.

YEHUDA: As for a man, a woman's wish to be an object creates anxiety. The difference is that her body perception prevents the possibility of giving part of her rather than all of her, thus resolving the anxiety.

ESTHER: Yes. To the man, she is all object.

YEHUDA: Not only to him; even to herself, when she feels threatened that someone wants all of her.

ESTHER: But on the other hand, she wants it too, everything . . .

YEHUDA: Now we're back to Freud: the anxiety is not only about being used, but about someone answering my wish to be used.

ESTHER: In that case, our culture's feminist evolution is effective, because it defines things for the woman. Feminism allows a woman to say, "I'm not a sexual object." In that way, it protects her from the threatening possibility of somebody wanting all of her and turning her into merely an object, or of managing to seduce somebody to want all of her. Feminism provides cultural defense, and then the woman can, if she acknowledges the concept and its importance, identify with it, and make it into a tool through which she can be less anxious.

YEHUDA: Right. That reminds me of what you said about the patient whose parents wanted him to study medicine.

ESTHER: Yes?

YEHUDA: Just as his parents wanted him to study medicine, so the man wants to sleep with the woman.

The patient's defensiveness is about the possibility of becoming his parents' object, a doctor object. The woman's defensiveness, her refusal, is toward being the man's sexual object, because that could obliterate her, obliterate her subjectivity.

ESTHER: Yes, the defensiveness is about the possibility of becoming an object.

YEHUDA: How do we return to subjectivity? By letting them choose whether or not to be an object.

ESTHER: Yes, exactly, by choosing. That's why feminism is teaching choice.

YEHUDA: Excellent. But just to remind ourselves, it's not a distinction between the genders or even the anatomy of men and women. It's the feminine or masculine *jouissance* that can be experienced by either gender.

ESTHER: And now that we've arrived at feminist thought, let's look at things from outside of Lacanian theory. Lacan's theory is very acceptable in the intellectual world we live in. Many philosophers study it, and its influence is widespread. And there, in a way, a woman remains outside of the theory, saying, hang on, please, this theory is appealing and impressive in its power to explain, but it's a man's theory, and there's a good chance this man is looking at women from within the Imaginary order. This isn't my argument, it's the starting point of Luce Irigaray's criticism of Lacanian theory. Irigaray is a Lacanian psychoanalyst who attended Lacan's seminars, and one of his best-known feminist critics. According to her, the psychoanalytic theory in general has always viewed women as flawed men (which is the origin of the concept of penis envy) – those who are not signified, because they lack.

To this criticism I would like to add my own: the concept of feminine *jouissance* expresses more than anything else, in my opinion, the Imaginary-masculine view of women: the Real, death, female *jouissance* – these are concepts that greatly overlap in Lacanian theory, and if something is missing, God can quickly be brought into the picture. Supposedly, there is something beyond words, including women, and all of this is shrouded in the mist of mystification. Moreover, Lacan himself speaks in Seminar 20 about female *jouissance* as something beyond words, comparing it to the mystical-spiritual experience. And of course, how could he not bring up the mystic Teresa of Avila – "You have only to go and look at Bernini's statue in Rome to understand immediately that she's coming." (This quote even appears on the cover of the Hebrew translation of his book.) Lacan only failed to remember that Teresa of Avila, the eternal orgasmer, is a statue, a statue of a climaxing woman that a male named Bernini made. Whether or not she is coming is evidence of nothing but the male imagination.

YEHUDA: Lacan himself agrees that he is limited to the male perspective. He has said it explicitly. He approached female psychoanalysts and asked them to speak from experience about female sexuality. He complained that women wouldn't talk about it, but certainly acknowledged his limitation as a man discussing the female experience. What you're arguing with regards to female *jouissance* – this concept is a result of Lacan's attempt to step outside of male fantasy. There is an imaginary male phantasm of what a woman is and what female *jouissance* is. He referred to this as The Woman. The feminine ideal, the *jouissance* ideal – he signified this with a strikethrough of the article "the" to emphasize that the woman as an ideal does not exist. That there is no prototype of the perfect woman as men imagine her. The phallic approach, which Lacan views as limited, divides the world into two: we men know who we are; the woman is everything else.

ESTHER: And therefore, if language is part of the Symbolic order, which is identified with the man (the father's name) than I, as a woman, remain outside of language, or, rather, fated to speak a language that is not my own.

YEHUDA: But this isn't about men and women. All women are part of the male field, and some men are part of the female field. The Oedipal drama, according to Freud, is in the transition of focus the child makes from his mother to his father. Lacan sees this as a myth, while the thing beneath the myth, to which the myth refers – is entrance into language. That's why the transition from mother to father, from femininity to masculinity, is a transition from the Real to the Symbolic. In this sense, the Symbolic is identified with the man, and the Real is identified with the woman. As soon as children become socialized and enter the Symbolic field, one could say they are in a phallic field regardless of their individual anatomy or their gender. The gender division, which is symbolic, is already a conceptualization that is by nature within the phallic field. This is just as relevant to men as it is to women. It reminds me of the difference between the lawful-rabbinical and the mystical aspects of religion. The rabbinate deals with laws, with permissions and prohibitions, with right and wrong. Meaning, it is in the phallic field. While mystics, whether male or female, seek what is beyond that field, beyond what can be defined through language. According to Lacan, mysticism is fundamentally based on female *jouissance*. Female *jouissance*, that is the name Lacan gives the mystical experience. That is the oceanic experience, like that of a fetus in the womb. Before entering language. Before Oedipus.

ESTHER: But why is it necessarily feminine? This distinction assumes that the essence of being female is in the "beyond," in that which has no words.

YEHUDA: I'll give you two reasons. One is female *jouissance* as a primordial state preceding the separation of the baby as an organ castrated from the mother's body. The second is a consequence of anatomical difference. Phallic nature is castration. Phallization is the name Lacan gave to entering language. Language dissects body and world. And there's another aspect to the reason that non-phallic *jouissance* is recognized as female *jouissance*: precisely because the body, without the distinction of a penis, without castration, represents a non-binary *jouissance*. A woman symbolizes the absence of castration. Lacan discusses male, or phallic *jouissance* as opposed to female or "Other" *jouissance*. It's a *jouissance* that exists among men and women, both anatomically and in terms of gender. A man can experience female *jouissance* and a woman can experience male *jouissance*. The reason Lacan tagged limited *jouissance* as "phallic" and limitless *jouissance* as "female" or "Other" is that this is the way things occur in patients' unconscious. For example, the psychoanalytic expression of limits is castration because this is how limits appear in the unconscious; in patients' dreams.

ESTHER: But neither men nor women would have words to describe an orgasm, so what's the difference?

YEHUDA: By virtue of being outside of words, an orgasm can be described as female *jouissance*.

ESTHER: So we have a loop here. We're back again at our starting point: everything outside of language is female *jouissance*. That's what you're saying. And I'm asking why everything "beyond" should be called "female."

YEHUDA: One could say that female *jouissance* is everything outside the bounds of patriarchy.

ESTHER: That's exactly the problem. If there is a patriarchy that refers to everything outside of its bounds as "woman," then language isn't neutral. That's the central argument of feminist criticism.

YEHUDA: If *jouissance* was tagged as being either "green" or "blue," would that solve the problem?

ESTHER: Yes!

YEHUDA: I think I understand. On the one hand, Lacanian theory quotes the unconscious of both men and women, which tags *jouissance* as either male or female. On the other hand, and especially since Lacanian theory has significant influence in our time, it also maintains a status quo. The gender conceptualization works as an interpretation that simultaneously describes and creates a reality. I think a feminist updating of Lacan's ideas would be most welcome not only for women.

Part 3: Anxiety and Theology

YEHUDA: Now I'd like to develop everything we've discussed into an even more complicated version.

ESTHER: Today??

YEHUDA: What's wrong? Are you getting anxious?

ESTHER: You want to add something even more complicated today??

YEHUDA: Yes, right this moment.

ESTHER: Are you serious?

YEHUDA: Yes.

ESTHER: You are not yet satisfied. All right then!

YEHUDA: Saying that whatever is inconceivable – such as the concept of infinity, such as wondrous coincidence, such as other inexplicable phenomena – comes from another dimension is precisely the anxiety of the inconceivable. It's an abstract version of everything we've said so far.

ESTHER: Yes. And then you can discuss secularity as a solution for this anxiety.

YEHUDA: No! On the contrary! Secularity is the reason for anxiety. Religion is the solution for anxiety, while secularity is its cause.

ESTHER: That is quite the contrary, as I see it.

YEHUDA: It depends on whether secularity is a religion in its own right.

ESTHER: Religion is the cause of the anxiety, and secularity is the solution. The opposite is true. You say "there is no God" and you're done. You've spared yourself the anxiety caused by infinity, which is unbearable for the mind, frustrating and confusing it endlessly.

YEHUDA: The lower God descends in culture; the higher anxiety rises. I'd like to remind you of the first chapter of this book, about being orphaned by God.

ESTHER: No way.

YEHUDA: God puts order into things; He tells us exactly what we ought to want.

ESTHER: No, no way.

YEHUDA: And without someone telling me what to want, where would I be?

ESTHER: Yehuda! We're back in theology, which is inevitable, but what are you –

YEHUDA: I'm not saying the solution is to become religious.

ESTHER: No, no, wait. The solution is to be clear. The solution is to choose! I'll bring you other sources that deal with this . . . Bion writes about it charmingly in his book *Second Thoughts*. He speaks about man's deterrence of infinity. Here:

"The idea of infinitude is prior to any idea of the finite [. . .] the human personality is aware of infinity, the 'oceanic feeling'. It became aware of limitation, presumably through physical and mental experience of itself and the sense of frustration. A number that is infinite, a sense of infinity, is replaced, say, by a sense of threeness. The sense that an infinite number of objects exists is replaced by a sense that only three objects exist, infinite space becomes finite space (Second Thoughts, P. 165)

The number, any number, is born out of infinity. Bion's basic assumption is that knowledge of the infinite precedes knowledge of the finite. Knowledge of the finite is a reduction of the infinite. Out of recurring encounters with the limitations of the senses and the resulting frustration, consciousness turns the infinite into the finite. The infinite "becomes three." The sense of infinity is frustrating because encountering it is encountering the unknowable, since our mental equipment is not suitable. It's probably analogous to Lacan's stance on the Real. That's why human consciousness picks the fruits of thought, the objects of knowledge, out of the infinite stream of experience. I assume these terms can replace Lacan's term, "the Symbolic order." All the while, consciousness has an a-priori familiarity with the infinite, along with a readiness to withstand the pain involved in this experience – a sense of infinity – meaning, bearing the knowledge that there aren't really any permanent, distinct objects, no final number of those, and that beneath the illusion of constancy there is a limitless stream of experience.

I'm mentioning all this because it directly touches upon the current discussion about the relationship between religion – and the assumption of God's existence – and anxiety. Bion discusses the frustration that arises when, to use the Lacanian term – the Real, which has no shape or name, touches the gates of consciousness. Then a conscious act of reduction takes place – the reduction of infinity to a trifecta or any other finite number. This act of reducing the infinite to a finite constitutes a solution for anxiety of the infinite. When Bion talks about psychoanalysis, for instance, or about the equipment necessary for a psychoanalyst, he asks for the equipment to be a sense of infinity and a tolerance to doubt. To me, that is one of his gems.

YEHUDA: Very nice.

ESTHER: It's lovely. It's the sentence that made me fall in love with Bion. His entire theory, which he calls "a theory of thinking," aspires toward this direction of tolerance of the sense of infinity and of doubt as the necessary condition, or mental equipment, necessary to truly know something. This statement is opposed to the intersubjective movement in psychoanalysis: When Mitchel talks about what happens in the room during psychoanalysis, he refers to two consciousnesses – actually, he says "two subjects" – that meet and collaborate. In a way, you, as a Lacanian, might agree with him on this matter. But it's very limited, the idea of an encounter of two minds, or two subjects, that meet. It's very limited. It's limited because through these subjects, cultures, history, and the future all meet, and a movement generates that is bigger than, you know, the "interpersonal space." Bion keeps talking about the presence of non-subjective intelligence. And his work, in spite of people's assumptions, does not have the flavor of new-age mysticism. Instead, it contains the presence of an ancient intelligence – everything that came before us. Now all of a sudden I'm sounding Jungian, and that isn't my intention. No, he talks about something even higher (I'm trying to phrase myself in a way you can accept, which is why I'm phrasing myself erroneously. I'm working against a foretold objection, trying to be strategic, so let me drop the strategy for a moment.): He talks about an infinity that is present in every encounter and about the possibility of a non-subjective state of mind in a clinician. What he's saying is that when you are working, you aren't a subject. You aren't a subject, and the thoughts you have are not your own. Rather, they are plucked from infinity, if you are in the right state of mind.

YEHUDA: I agree that the analyst is not a subject. Lacan is not inter-subjective. For him, intersubjectivity is an Imaginary limitation – two egos facing each other as in the mirror stage. I'll approach what you say from another direction. The Lacanian analyst's office is a structure containing two positions. The goal of treatment is to have the patient be a subject, and by positing themselves as objects, the analysts push patients into the only free space – the subject's sofa. They do that by inviting free associations and doing little beyond listening. In the process of transference, the patient projects all sorts of things onto the analyst, and the analyst can take it because they agree to be objects.

ESTHER: So, you're willing to be an object. You're an object while, in fact, you are a subject. Not exactly a subject: you use your intelligence. You aren't even a subject, you're a recipient for some intelligence, some nearly abstract being.

YEHUDA: In terms of the transference relationship, you're an object.

ESTHER: That's obvious. But what do you do on the inside?? It's clear enough you are an object for your patient. But how about deep inside? You aren't a subject.

YEHUDA: This is an attempt to be knowledge without a knower.

ESTHER: These are the very same words that Bion uses: "thoughts without a thinker."

YEHUDA: But the knowledge does work. It means being an object of the Symbolic order, of the chain of signifiers. To agree to be subjected to the patient's signifiers and let them speak through me.

ESTHER: Of course. Knowledge passes through the subject, but the subject (the psychoanalyst) is in a way – oh well, what can you do, we end up using concepts from Kabbalah and Chassidic thought – a conduit. You're a conduit, that's all. Bion says that in this work, your subjective part is a lie.

YEHUDA: The term "conduit" fits the position of the psychoanalyst, and the way in which the Symbolic field speaks through the psychoanalyst's throat is different from the counter-transference – a term that represents the biases the analysts bring with them.

ESTHER: Indeed, this is not counter-transference. It's another dimension of consciousness that allows you to see a patient's truth not from within your previous knowledge, not from within your memory, and not from within desire.

Chapter 12

More About *Jouissance,* and a Little About Depression

Jouissance is a state of nonexistence, which is why it inspires anxiety. At the kernel of every symptom is not only suffering and symbolic significance, but also pleasure. Yes, symptoms involve jouissance. It's hard to admit, but without admitting it, one cannot liberate themselves from the agony of the symptom.

One could view depression as a state of refusing to give something up. Ultimately, in order to recover from depression, one must give up that something.

And: a discussion of medicinal treatment.

ESTHER: We spoke about anxiety in our previous conversation. We discussed anxiety as Freud interpreted it and as Lacan did. According to Freud, generally speaking, anxiety is connected to something we're afraid to know, while Lacan says anxiety points to something much more fundamental: fear of anything nameless, anything we cannot explain – the Real. And the thing that connects these two kinds of anxiety: anxiety is always related to loss of identity, the undermining of identity, because the wish not to know appears when something doesn't suit the way a person identifies themselves. That's why we repress the thing that doesn't fit. And what does anxiety of the Real have to do with the undermining of identity?

YEHUDA: The Real means not existing. For Freud, first there is the human, and then the meanings they hold. If the meaning doesn't flatter them and they become aware of their disgusting drives, they will feel shame. In that case, anxiety is about knowledge that can lead to shame. This bears emphasizing: at the basis of Freud's perception is a person grasping knowledge, while for Lacan a person and their knowledge are one and the same. Meaning, the story isn't just a story we know or repress – it's a story in which we live. The anxiety is not only the alarm signal that there is "something" we don't want to know, but about a fuller sobering: a sobering from living this story. If this is sobering, then life as we've known it falls apart. That means that far on the horizon of the anxiety attack, is a trauma, the threat of nonexistence. And Freud didn't completely understand trauma. He was a positivist, which is why he didn't realize that the story is life itself, because life and the story

DOI: 10.4324/9781003342458-12

are one and the same – and trauma is the dismantling of life, because life falls apart when the story falls apart, upon sobering.

ESTHER: Meaning, we cannot separate the story from life. We live a life that tells our story, and so the dismantling of the story is the dismantling of life.

YEHUDA: Indeed. Freud's alternative to the ideal story is the true, shameful one. In addition to Freud, Lacan's alternative to the story – any story – is the state of being outside of the story, meaning – not being.

ESTHER: As a sidebar, let me say that, apropos our discussion of anxiety regarding trauma, or anxiety of the Real, I'd like to remind you that we discussed *jouissance*. That term still isn't clear enough to me. We discussed female *jouissance* as Real or close to Real, and as such it can evoke anxiety. That led us to the subject of *jouissance* in general.

YEHUDA: In that case, let's discuss the relationship between anxiety and *jouissance*: the Freudian anxiety contains the fear of knowing about the drive, along with the fear that the drive will take effect and entail prices and damages and breaking prohibitions. This is, then, not only a fear of knowing about the drive, but a fear of being tempted by it. Living the drive is a state of *jouissance*. According to Lacan, *jouissance* is not only shameful – as it is according to Freud – but annihilating. Losing one's senses means no longer existing. And when existence is difficult, addiction to *jouissance* is tempting: not existing is tempting. Another thing we can say about this term – and this is how it might be different from "pleasure" or "enjoyment" – is that it involves suffering.

ESTHER: How so?

YEHUDA: To understand this, we first need to understand Lacan's interpretation of Freud's "Beyond the Pleasure Principle." Simple animalistic pleasure means balance, homeostasis, tranquility. Freud mistakenly used the term "Nirvana." But since language turns the relationship between existent and nonexistent arbitrary – allowing statements such as "I have no appetite" rather than just "I have no food," meaning, "The absence is absent." The situation created is one in which the nonexistent has a kind of existence that can be held onto, providing a sort of satisfaction. This is how we differ from animals. Animals seek tranquility. They're either satiated, and then they are tranquil, or they are hungry, and then tense. For humankind, things are different: since people live in language, they can turn the nonexistent into existence. They can say, "I have an appetite," and then the invigoration and the tension stemming from a lack of food take on the status of satisfaction; the status of something that exists. Language can turn the experience of desire into one of satisfaction. Simple, organic satisfaction, like the physical release experienced in orgasm or satiation after a meal. It can be called "enjoyment." The satisfaction involved in organic-level experience is intertwined with stress, such as during appetite – that is a paradoxical satisfaction that involves suffering on the organic level. That's one way to explain the term "*jouissance*."

ESTHER: But that is an explanation of desire, not of *jouissance* . . . "Living the drive," those are the words you use to define *jouissance*. Why does *jouissance*, meaning, "living the drive," involve agony?

YEHUDA: Because the experience of satisfaction – that satisfaction which is not organic satiation, but is intertwined with the existence of desire, as absurd as it might sound – does not satisfy a person: one can eat to satiation and then keep on eating. Most of us continue eating after we are already full, because it tastes good. Meaning, we no longer seek out homeostasis – the complete lack of stress – like other animals. Human satisfaction is, in fact, a sustained stress of desire. Language reshuffles the cards with a desire-satisfaction dialectic.

ESTHER: In that case, *jouissance* isn't essentially connected to agony, but to always wanting more.

YEHUDA: True. The "I Want more" – that is the agony of *jouissance*. That's why the more accurate term would be "excess *jouissance*."

ESTHER: The "I want more!"

YEHUDA: Yes. That's one way to look at it; a simpler way. That is the point where we choose to over-stimulate ourselves. Sometimes we are exposed to over-stimulation against our will – such as in traumatic events. And that creates an intense experience. There is something pleasurable in the intensity of the experience that we want to recreate, which is why trauma recreates itself – because its over-stimulation is seductive. A patient could say – "I made an anxiety attack." They created it. They could also say, "Ever since my anxiety went away, something's been missing." There was a *jouissance* that they miss.

ESTHER: Does *jouissance* always appear in a symptom? Is it always connected to a symptom?

YEHUDA: The symptom is a way of experiencing *jouissance*.

ESTHER: But it's a *certain* way of experiencing it. The symptom attaches something else to the *jouissance* . . .

YEHUDA: Let's take, for example, a symptom such as Trichotillomania – the urge to pull out one's hair. One grabs the hair and pulls it slowly – feeling the stress – and then the hair pops out of the scalp – a climax – a moment of tranquility and release. Meaning, there is a sexual experience undergone through pulling out the hair. That is the cycle of *jouissance*, stress, and release.

One can explain this symptom using its specific meaning: the father of the girl who suffers of Trichotillomania hides his baldness with the "comb-over" method. By doing this, he is actualizing a message of denying a lack. Lack has no place in the family, and the girl presents her unconscious protest through Trichotillomania. The symptom positions itself around the fact that the father chooses to disguise his lack. The family also happens to have some Holocaust trauma they don't speak of. You could interpret that. You could tell the girl, "You're insisting on revealing the faults the family is trying to hide." And then it turns out that pulling out the hair is merely a symbol for something else – the dilemma of whether or not to disguise. Yet the interpretation, finding the meaning of the symptom, won't necessarily be enough to get her to give up pulling out her hair, because the experience of *jouissance* brought on by pulling out the hair won't let up. There is something beyond meaning; there is raw pleasure.

ESTHER: Pleasure that is beyond meaning!

YEHUDA: Pleasure that is beyond meaning. And after we've finished emptying the symptom of any meaning it carried, it still persists, because the kernel of the symptom underneath the meaning that holds it is a physical *jouissance*. Once its acknowledged, the subject can choose whether or not to give it up. How can you give up something if you don't know it exists? Having emptied out all other meanings that held it? And then – after you acknowledge the pleasure you derive from the symptom – it's only a question of being conscious of the pleasure and choosing whether or not to give it up.

ESTHER: I want to clarify one last thing: I thought, probably mistakenly, that a symptom is created in order to camouflage *jouissance*. But I'm wrong. A symptom is created because it expresses meaning, and alongside this expression of meaning there is also *jouissance*.

YEHUDA: Yes. It's hard to say what is alongside what. If anything, the Symbolic is alongside the Real. The main thing is the real nucleus of *jouissance*, not the Symbolic envelope of meaning. But we must pass through the Symbolic envelope of meaning in order to arrive at the real *jouissance*.

ESTHER: Regarding *jouissance* – clinically, there's nothing we can do beyond saying, "But you also enjoy it."

YEHUDA: "You must choose either to identify with it or give it up."

ESTHER: As always.

YEHUDA: Like every fifth square of chocolate. The complicated thing is realizing that it's chocolate, because it doesn't look like chocolate, it looks like a nightmare. And yet – to detect the pleasure in it. Then we can start treating it like chocolate and negotiating whether or not to give it up. What exposes the *jouissance* of the symptom is taking apart the envelope of meaning.

ESTHER: All right. That's it. We've done this quick discussion of *jouissance* that was very interesting. Now let's talk about depression.

YEHUDA: Depression, which must be more complicated than everything else.

ESTHER: More than anxiety?

YEHUDA: Yes.

ESTHER: Yes?

YEHUDA: Yes indeed. Because anxiety entails a subject; someone to work with. There is vitality in anxiety. What anxiety and depression have in common is that both involve a refusal to give up the object. Anxiety often takes form as anguish, which is an experience of excess, an excess of something we refuse to give up. One of the most basic interpretations of anxiety of drives has to do with an anxiety about the incestuous drive, the drive to return to the womb, the yearning to become somebody else's object. Anxiety is a state in which I fear being somebody's object. But I am the one refusing to give up the thing that blocks me. That's where anxiety lies: I won't give up the object, and therefore cannot set myself free. Depression is also about not giving up the object. But since the object is lost, I lose myself right after it.

ESTHER: Freud, *Mourning and Melancholia.*

YEHUDA: Precisely, precisely. That's the principle of depression. Lacan quotes Shakespeare, who wrote that Hamlet jumped into the grave after Ophelia. Meaning, he refused to part from the object –

ESTHER: The dead object.

YEHUDA: The dead object. And the solution is mourning, grieving, turning the dead into a symbol that can live on, which is *Totem and Taboo*: turning the dead into a symbol. That's one way to approach depression.

ESTHER: Let's open this up. Are there other ways to talk about depression? Other types of depression?

YEHUDA: We can talk about different types of depression in the context of clinical constructs: hysteria, obsession, perversion, psychosis. You could ask how each of these constitutes a style of the myth that constructs a subject with desire. There is the obsessive strategy, there is the hysterical strategy. The strategies answer the question of how one can exist as a subject with desire. Depression is a situation in which strategy doesn't work and therefore desire doesn't take place. Depression is the lack of desire.

ESTHER: So we have two main points.

YEHUDA: Yes.

ESTHER: In that case, we are now discussing the first point: dying after an object dies, that one cannot give up.

YEHUDA: Yes.

ESTHER: We're not only talking about someone dealing with actual death, of course. We're also talking about quitting cigarettes, or any other kind of parting.

YEHUDA: Yes.

ESTHER: And also, about someone's self-image.

YEHUDA: Everything. Anything. If there is a depression diagnosis, the immediate question is, "What is the person refusing to give up?"

ESTHER: The question is, what is the thing the person is refusing to give up.

YEHUDA: What's been lost, where the loss was supposedly accepted? It's a kind of despair: I won't live without it. How do we treat that?

ESTHER: How?

YEHUDA: This is how: We ask questions. How come you're still alive? Why do you choose to keep on living? Meaning, we point to the fact that this person isn't yet in the grave. What is their choice? To live.

ESTHER: Okay. So this is the end of the discussion, right?

YEHUDA: The discussion is over, indeed. But this is precisely what makes depression such a difficult symptom to work with, because we quickly arrive at this point: that's it, what more is there to say? We could say that depression has medical aspects. There is organic depression. It can appear as a side effect of diabetes, Parkinson's, postpartum . . . And even if there is a psychological aspect – because getting Parkinson's is naturally upsetting – there is also an organic aspect: serotonin levels drop, dopamine levels drop.

ESTHER: In these cases, I recommend medication.

YEHUDA: Right.

ESTHER: and then I help the patient go through the biological, organic crisis, and get back up on their feet. I don't get sentimental or worked up about it, and what I have to treat is the question of why the patient is refusing to accept medicinal treatment. And in this respect, one prominent thing about depression, as opposed to other disorders, is the way people hold onto it.

YEHUDA: I used to have a patient who called it "cuddling up with depression."

ESTHER: Of course.

YEHUDA: And that's *jouissance*.

ESTHER: Of course! So I see *jouissance* before me and I remain indifferent. I'm not a part of it.

YEHUDA: That's why, if a person suffering from depression reads this book and wants to find some useful information, the first question we recommend asking themselves is: Why am I not asking for help? Why am I not seeking therapy? Why am I not contacting a psychiatrist for medication? When I ask these questions, I'm not trying to urge them to do these things. I'm genuinely asking why. Try to answer these questions. The answers will likely be, "Because it's beneath me," "Because I'm afraid of becoming addicted," "Because what would people say," "Because it means I'm crazy." All of your biases about medication. These biases are the meanings that create depression. You might need medication. You might take it and feel better and then give that up, too. Another option is that you've taken medication before and it didn't help, or that you vehemently refuse to take medication and still ask what could be the meaning of this depression. If that is the case, search for the thing you've lost but cannot give up, and ask yourself why you can't give it up. What is the thing you cannot let go of, and why? Which characters play a part in the drama that stops you from letting go? Another question is whether you can recognize the pleasure, the cuddling, the self-pity, the expectation to be served, the depression as a form of protest you cannot give up until somebody notices the way you're being wronged. If the depression is a message, then start using your words. Figure out who this message is aimed at. But if you can't even understand this depression, how should the person you're directing it at understand it?

ESTHER: Then why is it hard to treat depression? You sound very clear and consistent . . .

YEHUDA: A further step is necessary in order to have a person here, a partner, someone to talk to. In anxiety, in symptoms, there is someone to talk to, but depression positions a patient in a demanded place: they have to be the active ones, which is the hard part. "Active" not in the sense of taking action. It's the feeling of somebody making demands of you; someone you must satisfy.

ESTHER: And then you're stuck in the role they give you – the work of clarification, and then giving up depression, is yours, not theirs.

YEHUDA: In the Lacanian technique, the length of the session is not predetermined but depends on the content. The idea that the story would reach its natural point at the fiftieth minute makes no sense. The story will reach its natural point in its own time, typically, in my experience, somewhere between twenty and forty minutes. Sometimes the patient has nothing to say, perhaps because they are depressed, or for other reasons. They've got nothing to say but expect to be put into action, and then it's possible, in a relatively short amount of time, to end the session. That can certainly anger the patient, and anger is not depression.

ESTHER: Anger is lively.

YEHUDA: And then you could say to the patient, "Your anger tells me there is something you want." That'll only happen during the next session. They can be angry for a full week. "Your anger tells me there's something you want. What is the thing you want?"

ESTHER: "For you to help me." That's what they'll say.

YEHUDA: "What is the thing you want me to help you achieve? How important it is to you to get over your depression? How much are you willing to invest in that? Are you willing to give up your biases and take medication? Are you willing to work out for two hours a day? Are you willing to volunteer with the less fortunate and feel some compassion?"

ESTHER: Wonderful. See? Here's the thing. It's about the anticipation – the demand, to use your words – that you be the infinite container, and you decline. Indeed, it depends on who you work with, because, as you said, "There's nobody to work with, I need the patient to be here." But, to generalize, depression is a type of conspiracy, one that has a certain hysterical nature, because it is shaped as a demand, addressing the other with a complaint from the start: "My wellbeing depends on you." That is the stance one eventually arrives at, in cases of depression. But here's a question: we say that depression is the result of a refusal to give up the object. Someone comes to you for treatment and you become the object, and then they don't give you up and keep trying to make demands of you.

YEHUDA: But that's only in the hysterical context. Some depressions have an obsessive background.

ESTHER: And what does it look like then?

YEHUDA: The obsessive strategy to sustain desire is to be ordered: someone else demands of me the thing I want to get from myself. That's why I pay a personal trainer to force me to do what I actually want to do, and when I forget that I'm paying her I feel that she's being bossy and I complain to her. Then she reminds me that I pay her, and that's why I'm the boss and she is only my representative. And then I relax and obey the orders I consciously asked for. As an obsessive, I repress the setup where I wanted to be demanded, and then I feel as if someone is abusing me and bossing me around without realizing I myself had envisioned it, ordered it, created it, and chose the right person for the job. And my bitterness is the denial of the fact that I made a choice. In obsessive depression, there is no one to get me moving. The trick of self-activation through another doesn't work, and so I don't move. That's the depression. Or the fact that it's a choice is unconscious, and then I feel oppressed by this fascist whom I forgot I myself had recruited and who keeps telling me I'm not good enough, and that's another reason to get depressed.

The starting-off point of the obsessive technique is to be activated by a command. This is done in order to avoid acting out of choice. Acting out of choice comes at a price, but obeying a command has no price. There might be a punishment if one does not obey the command, but punishment is not the same as price. When a police officer gives you a ticket for driving without a seatbelt, they are the commanders. They demand and are obeyed, or else there is punishment. This all is meant to conceal the choice of risking death by a car accident. The obsessive strategy is to be oppressed by a dictator. It is intended to avoid dealing with the lack, the price of choice. And now I'd like to make a connection to something we spoke about earlier: depression, as we said, appears when there is something one won't give up. Just like in *Mourning and Melancholia*, when people refuse to part with the dead. You could apply this to any choice. Any choice has two options, and if you won't give up one for the sake of another, you'll be depressed for not fulfilling a desire, because you refuse to give up anything. You've managed to recruit some imaginary character to rip the thing out of your hands and leave you with only one choice? Great, that was your way of giving up the thing. You refuse this command? Then you fail to give up the thing. You experience this command as something that erases you? Once again, depression.

Now let's move on to a psychotic construct. The psychotic can live in a delusion of being the messiah, of being fated to greatness. They're living in a story that offers a mission, a desire, honor, and belonging. When they take anti-psychotic drugs, they can rid themselves of the delusion, but when they rid themselves of the delusion (meaning, of this story that sustains the mission, the belonging, and the honor) they remain without a myth that sustains desire. And then post-psychotic-attack depression appears. I say this because the structure, psychotic or otherwise, remains.

ESTHER: That's a good reason to be depressed. It's loss of meaning. Then what can you offer as their clinician?

YEHUDA: I must help them find a myth in which to live. Let's see what kind of meaning we can sustain without delusion. At first, the meaning will be coming to treatment. "I want you to come in three times a week. Your mission is to tell me how you're feeling." They prepare for this task and already they have a job in the world. If, in addition, the post-psychotic patient has something to teach the clinician, it would be even better. If they can teach the clinician history, or computer science – anything they know about and the clinician doesn't – that gives them a job in the world.

ESTHER: Just like that.

YEHUDA: Yes! Now let's move on to the perverted construct. Here, depression is connected to the loss of pleasure. If, for some organic reason, they can't sustain the pleasure for which they live – because the pervert lives under the banner, "I take pleasure, therefore I am" – if they cannot take pleasure, they will get depressed, which is, more or less, the only way they'd ever come into treatment, because they have no other reason.

ESTHER: Can we talk about a post-perverted state?

YEHUDA: The personality structure does not change. Concerning the pervert, this is the state of one who still has a perverse personality structure but can no longer perform the perverted act. The depression of the perverted stems from the fact that *jouissance* is no longer available for different reasons of choice or coercion, chemical castration or old age. All sorts of reasons.

ESTHER: Well, it happens.

YEHUDA: And then they must learn to enjoy desire; to try and develop their neurotic side.

ESTHER: Okay. Now let's put things in order. In depression, we always have the problem of giving up an object, no matter which structure we're discussing.

YEHUDA: The conclusion regarding the question of how to live a depression-free life: make sure you have a myth to live by, even if you know it's just a myth. If you truly believe in God and are part of a religious community, you are fairly protected against depression, because you live in a myth. If this faith is shaken, the risk of depression might arise. I'm talking about "religion" on the most general level: it can be socialism or nationalism, family or romance – any ideology. The outlier in this context is an oppressive myth such as a firm belief in excessive morality. That kind of myth cannot prevent depression, due to its oppressive nature to begin with.

If one is so sober – and this is where we started our conversations, with the question of whether sobriety takes the spark out of life – that they no longer know how to invent a life and live it, then depression is an invitation for that.

ESTHER: An invitation to invent a life to live.

Chapter 13

Different Reasons for Depression

What causes a person to lose their desire? There is a variety of reasons. Sometimes they refuse to risk getting frustrated again because in the past they have agreed to yearn over and over again, experiencing disappointment over and over again, and now refuse to take the risk of disappointment once more. Another possibility is that their desire is forbidden. If it still exists but they mustn't know about it, anxiety develops, and if it cannot exist at all then they remain without desire, which creates depression.

This chapter will also discuss the relationship between depression and clinical structures (hysteria, obsession, perversion, psychosis). We distinguish depression as a function of a structure and depression that is not. "Function of a structure" means a lack is created through one of three strategies.

But for an orphan who has lost their mother, it isn't about a strategy for creating desire, but about the difficulty of accepting a loss.

ESTHER: We are in the last third of the book, Yehuda.

YEHUDA: Yes, we're coming toward the end.

ESTHER: In terms of topics, we're almost finished. All we have left to talk about is love, depression, and death.

YEHUDA: But what comes first, love or depression? We still need to complete our discussion of depression.

ESTHER: There's anxiety, then depression, then love, then death. It's best to have love just before death, isn't it?

YEHUDA: Absolutely. Let's go!

ESTHER: We spoke about anxiety in the previous chapter. Among other things, we talked about anxiety as connected to the Real. In this context, it's interesting to note that most antidepressant medication also treat anxiety. There is a connection – which one could say is biological, or Real, in the sense that it exists in the organic aspect – between depression and anxiety.

YEHUDA: Yes. The Lacanian logic about the relationship between depression and anxiety is one whose starting point is desire: depression is a state of lack of desire, while anxiety is a state in which desire is undefined, unchanneled,

DOI: 10.4324/9781003342458-13

unnamed. If it only had a name, if only the drive could be anchored by a fetish, we could take pleasure in it rather than let it circulate within the body like an energy with no outlet. The thing anxiety and depression have in common is that they are both connected to desire. One is confusion around desire, which is anxiety. The other is a lack of desire, which is depression.

ESTHER: What causes a person to lose their desire?

YEHUDA: There is a variety of reasons. Sometimes they refuse to risk getting frustrated again because in the past they have agreed to yearn over and over again, experiencing disappointment over and over again, so they say: I won't risk being disappointed once more, I won't yearn anymore. Another possibility is that their desire is forbidden. If it still exists but they mustn't know about it, anxiety develops. If it's so forbidden that it cannot exist at all, not even suppressed, but must be annihilated, along with the annihilation of its holder, then they remain without desire, which creates depression.

ESTHER: So, it could be that a person whose value system forbids feeling attracted to children, for example, will experience a conflict. I'm talking about inner conflict according to Freud's structural model.

YEHUDA: Correct.

ESTHER: But he's a pedophile and doesn't care about anything else, so he'll just get depressed. Meaning, his desire will be oppressed.

YEHUDA: Right. And then not only will he not be a pedophile, but he won't be any kind of "phile" (meaning "love" in Greek). So he'll get depressed, because he'll feel no desire toward anything. The pharmacological form of this is the depression which is a side effect of the chemical castration of sexual offenders.

ESTHER: So how could you help a person who harbors a desire that is forbidden or harmful?

YEHUDA: By making it unforbidden in his own eyes. Indeed, it is forbidden to fulfil, but why should it be forbidden to feel?

ESTHER: Okay.

YEHUDA: Pedophilia is not the drive itself but the act, the fulfilment. Some people view the very existence of the drives themselves as illegal. The perspective that takes blame for the mere existence of the drive, that can change:

ESTHER: I have a patient whose own perversion disgusts him.

YEHUDA: I think disgust in this case is a way to talk about criticism. He can't live peacefully with his own drives. The question is whether one can live at peace with the existence of the drive that is not fulfilled.

ESTHER: Their mere existence. So it's an example of the suppression of a drive.

YEHUDA: And there's another reason for depression, which is loss. Like in the Hamlet example, where rather than mourn Ophelia, he follows her into the grave.

ESTHER: To be or not to be.

YEHUDA: To be or not to be a subject. To be a subject means remaining in lack when the lost thing is gone. And "not to be" is to cling to the lost object, even if originally that is the mother whose womb is entered.

ESTHER: Which is a psychotic choice.

YEHUDA: Yes.

ESTHER: In that case, "not to be" is not to be a subject, meaning not to give up unity with the object. Not to be a subject means not to give up the thing that can be the petit-a object in the psychotic case, or anything else you refuse to give up. And when it's lost, you get lost along with it.

YEHUDA: Right. Another way of saying the same thing would be: if you refuse to give up the object, you don't have the lack that is the foundation of desire.

ESTHER: Okay! That's well-organized from a logical point of view. That's how we can understand depression.

YEHUDA: And nevertheless, let me point this out: I think that depression contains more of an organic emphasis than other disorders. Depression can be more a side effect of a physical problem than other psychological phenomena.

ESTHER: Why do you wish to point that out?

YEHUDA: It's been my experience. It's possible that there are clinicians better than me in treating depression without medication, but in my experience, psychological treatment is not as powerful for depression as it is for other disorders. You thought differently when we discussed it . . .

ESTHER: Indeed, in our previous conversation I spoke about a different feeling of mine. I don't acquiesce to my patients' request for pity. Rather, I stay quite calm and unmoved by it, and ultimately many of them get over their depression and choose desire. I assume this happens because I refuse to acquiesce to a very specific type of pity they request.

YEHUDA: So let's talk about pity as a kind of depression medication.

ESTHER: Yes, let's talk about that. But first I'd like to bring up the question of whether we can actually talk about depression in a general way, or if we ought to talk about different kinds of depression. You've already done the first round of categorization when you distinguished between organic and inorganic depression. And I'm starting to think about other possible categorizations, because there is a wide arc of symptoms we refer to by a single name. I was concerned with that after our previous conversation. At the extreme are suicidal attempts, and there is a question about the possibility of explaining a suicidal act and the nature of the depression that preceded it. That's why I ask if we're talking about one thing or three or five things, when we talk about depression.

YEHUDA: I listened to a talk by a woman who had a concussion and developed an instant, organic depression. Parkinson's also contains an element of organic depression, as does postpartum hormonal disorder. That's why I'm reluctant to say everything is psychological. Instead, I will say that there are different types of organic depression. And then physical symptoms would be apparent too (lackluster mood, lack of appetite, overtiredness, excessive sleep or sleep deprivation), while mental symptoms, such as mood swings, would not constitute a main part of the picture.

ESTHER: And yet I still believe we ought to think of other categories.

YEHUDA: We've already discussed clinical structures as categories.

ESTHER: Okay, that's exactly what I was going to say. If I was one of the people writing the DSM, the psychiatric guide for the diagnosis of psychological disorders, would I create a category named "Depressive Personality Disorder?" Maybe one could say there is a personality type that contains a depressive dimension. Perhaps there are some people for whom you could say depression is just part of their personality.

YEHUDA: Depression is not a structure, because a structure is what sustains desire and depression is a state of lack of desire. The clinical structures – psychosis, perversion, and the two types of neurosis – hysteria and obsession – are actually strategies intended to sustain a myth that upholds desire. The psychotic myth doesn't work well. There is no myth there, and that's the problem. There is no lack.

ESTHER: I'm a king, I'm whole – that's the myth.

YEHUDA: Right, exactly. That's why the psychotic believes that only the other has lacked. And because they lack, they try to take something away from me. That's where paranoia begins. As for the pervert: their desire is pain and they must fill it up with pleasure. They cannot enjoy the existence of the lack. They have a lack but they don't enjoy it. That's why our emphasis in the case of perversion is that depression will develop when there is no possibility of indulging in pleasure. The loss of pleasure will cause depression, whether it occurs because he is imprisoned for his perversion –

ESTHER: Or because he's old.

YEHUDA: Or because his libido runs out and he can no longer take pleasure in the things he once did. Then depression occurs, and there's also a chance that the perverted person will come to treatment. On the other hand, there is the hysterical strategy for constructing a lack that allows desire: I don't have it because I'm deprived. Then the person has to come up with a story of why they lack. The hysterical story is "I don't have it because I'm deprived," and one can be so deprived that they become depressed. Or there is no possibility of deprivation, and therefore no desiring because there is no foundation for desire, no foundation for lack. This will also lead to depression, over not being allowed to be deprived, meaning – desirous. The obsessive utilizes the same trick, but for them, rather than being deprived, like the hysterical, they live under the weight of a decree, a prohibition. Then they deprive themselves of all pleasures, because everything is forbidden. They might reach the point of depression, either because they are living in a story according to which the demand directed at them is depressing, or because they've got no story in which to live, no story in which something is demanded of them, inspiring desire. Their trick in order to want, to generate desire, is to want what is forbidden. That's why, when everything is allowed, they've got no reason to want. This is another way for depression to occur in an obsessive structure.

ESTHER: Meaning, if this is a man who cheats on his wife, leading to divorce, then now everything is allowed, but it loses its flavor.

YEHUDA: Yes. Yes. If it isn't forbidden, there is no appeal. That's why depression will appear in clinical structures either as a side effect of the clinical structure or as a side effect of the fact that the clinical structure does not work as the desire strategy.

ESTHER: Wait, explain that again please.

YEHUDA: One of two possibilities. The first: depression occurs because, to take the hysterical for instance –

ESTHER: He doesn't receive or the world won't give him, is that what you're saying?

YEHUDA: The first possibility is that depression occurs because the person feels deprived.

ESTHER: Yes.

YEHUDA: The second possibility is that he is not deprived and desiring within deprivation is not possible, and there is no alternative, and then depression occurs. For example, a patient who was depressed because she couldn't find a partner, and in her hysterical experience love was something to desire, not something to fulfil. That's why, when it did come true, her depression just switched causes: rather than depression due to loneliness she felt depressed due to lack of desire. Her desire could sustain itself as long as its object was unattainable. But she couldn't desire an existing partner, could only desire him when he was gone. Once he existed, her desire disappeared and depression appeared. Would she be able to learn how to desire him in his presence? That's the question. If so, she would be able to overcome her depression.

ESTHER: You get everything you've ever wanted your entire life, and this makes you depressed.

YEHUDA: Right. It's called –

ESTHER: Someone wants to be a writer. They are declared a writer, and they become depressed! Unbelievable!

YEHUDA: It's called Postdoc Depression.

ESTHER: Is that true?!

YEHUDA: It happens when you're at the point after your wish comes true, like after obtaining your doctorate.

ESTHER: And then?

YEHUDA: And then you are without wishes.

ESTHER: Exactly. For a moment. If only for a moment.

YEHUDA: Yes, until a new wish comes together, you're depressed. It's also called anticlimax.

ESTHER: Yes, yes . . . okay; this is a meaningful addition to understanding depression in the context of structures. I had a patient that I think I didn't understand, and that's connected. As we said in previous chapters, people create the theatre of their lives according to their structures. They actually create the drama at the end of which they come out deprived. There are all sorts of ways to do that. For instance, if you go into business with people who are obviously going to end up screwing you over, you create –

YEHUDA: We've said it before and we'll say it again: there are three strategies for constructing reality to suit one's structure: you either choose the right people for the job, or you provoke them so much that they become the right people for the job, or you imagine they're the right people for the job.

ESTHER: Okay. So let's say the patient I'm talking about was really good at it. That means he's depressed all the time, because he's constantly deprived and screwed over, having arranged this situation with impressive skill. I think he uses all three strategies, and he ends up being continuously depressed, a depression inherent in his life.

YEHUDA: Right. But I would say it's more than inherent; its depression serving as proof of the fictitious reality: I'm depressed therefore my deprivation is real, otherwise I wouldn't be depressed. Depression is the proof of my deprivation, and the fact that I'm deprived is proof of my lack. I lack, therefore I am.

ESTHER: Since the goal is "I lack, therefore I am" – it can't be a very acute depression. Because if it's depression intended to prove my lack, then I am a little bit of a subject.

YEHUDA: Right. A more acute depression will occur if and when they cannot position themselves as deprived. It will be more of a psychotic depression. Melancholia. Without even a complaint.

ESTHER: That's it!

YEHUDA: They have no desire outside of deprivation. Without deprivation, they have no desire. This goes back to our discussion of anxiety. We could talk about positivist conceptualization of depression or anxiety a la Freud, and on the other hand about postmodern or Lacanian conceptualization of depression or anxiety. "Freudian" depression results from the feeling that "I'm being deprived" and Freudian anxiety is directed at the knowledge that I enjoy it. The Lacanian depression occurs before the story in which I'm being deprived falls apart, and anxiety is the fear that it might fall apart.

ESTHER: Okay. In this case, you aren't actually treating the depression but rather the structure. You are treating the need to be deprived; the choice to be deprived.

YEHUDA: Correct.

ESTHER: Not the depression.

YEHUDA: Right.

ESTHER: When do you treat the depression?

YEHUDA: In situations of loss, when a separation from the lost object did not occur yet even though the object is lost.

ESTHER: Meaning, when there is trauma or real loss –

YEHUDA: When there is real loss.

ESTHER: Separation, marriage, divorce, death –

YEHUDA: Yes, yes, or when someone has a hope of becoming something and they realize it isn't going to happen.

ESTHER: Meaning, when there's a trigger –

YEHUDA: Even a future hope that disappears is a loss. If you could put your finger on loss –

ESTHER: Then you work with that.

YEHUDA: Then I work with that.

ESTHER: And if there is no such trigger but rather something chronic, meaning, someone who makes sure to be deprived and therefore chronically depressed –

YEHUDA: Then I try to detect the foundation of the depression: deprivation, prohibition, guilt, denial of drives. I try to find the foundation. Sometimes there is none.

ESTHER: In a sense, we are talking about the same thing, because even when we're talking about deprivation, we're talking about loss. The only difference is that it is an early loss. If it's a patient who lost his mother at age fourteen, and ever since life proves to him over and over again that this loss has no repair. In this case, you'd also work with the loss, even though –

YEHUDA: But it isn't a structure, it's a loss. A structure happens when one invents the loss in order to exist in desire.

ESTHER: Okay.

YEHUDA: That isn't real loss.

ESTHER: Let's argue about that for a moment, all right?

YEHUDA: Yes.

ESTHER: If I told you he lost his mother at age three, would that make any difference?

YEHUDA: No.

ESTHER: In our first chapter, which I think is a wonderful chapter, and dealt with orphanhood, you said something that stayed with me: you said that losing a father is a disaster but not a deprivation. That's what you said. To me, that's categorical. It makes all the difference. Now, loss creates deprivation anyway. The deprivation is created along with the loss. That's exactly my point: that deprivation and depression are really the same thing.

YEHUDA: The question is, what is the goal. A person who loses his mother wants his mother back. But some want to miss their mothers while they are still alive, and will therefore imagine themselves as deprived. Scratch that, let me find a better way to express this idea.

ESTHER: No, that's good, it's great!

YEHUDA: The hysterical state is not based on a history of deprivation, but on a fantasy of deprivation that allows desire. That's why I would use different approaches with the mourner and the hysterical. To the mourner – even if he lost his mother thirty years ago – I would say, it's time to say goodbye and move on. To the hysterical I would say, why are you living in a fantasy of missing something to the point of deprivation? It's an invention, an imagination. One classic example of hysteria is a woman defining herself through what she lacks: "I have no penis, therefore I'm a woman." Freud's notion of penis envy.

ESTHER: Right.

YEHUDA: But she doesn't truly want a penis; she wants a definition of femininity. The lack of a penis is proof that she's a woman. She needs a different proof. At the same time, a man might feel like he doesn't have a penis, like he "isn't man enough." And what he wants isn't to say, "I have no penis; therefore, I am a woman." He wants to say, "I'm lacking a signifier of masculinity." With this patient, I would work to figure out why he feels this way. I wouldn't deal with "Why do you insist your penis is gone" but rather with, "Let's find it." For example, if his father didn't give him –

ESTHER: That's the same thing.

YEHUDA: The question is, what is the motivation. The question is whether the motivation is to be –

ESTHER: To define yourself through what you don't have.

YEHUDA: Or if the goal is to have it. If a mourner's goal is to bring his mother back to life, I won't tell him he insists on maintaining her as gone, but agree with him that she's gone and suggest completing the mourning process.

ESTHER: Yes.

YEHUDA: It's a loss; a real loss that must be accepted. When a woman says, "I have no penis, therefore I am a woman" – she is inventing a loss for the sake of her definition as a woman. God made her just as she is. Nothing is missing, and she is the one who chooses to see herself as lacking.

ESTHER: Shall I tell you what the two cases have in common?

YEHUDA: Yes.

ESTHER: I see more similarities than differences between them. The dialectic you are referring to is a dialectic of have and have not. You say: some people cling to the lack and define themselves through it. The depressive person who lost his mother defines himself through his lack of a mother. The woman defines herself through her lack of a penis. It doesn't matter what the missing piece is – something is missing.

YEHUDA: I'm not sure –

ESTHER: That's exactly my problem.

YEHUDA: I'm not sure the orphan defines himself by his lack. He suffers the depression of loss. I'm not sure he uses this to reach self-definition.

ESTHER: Not "to reach self-definition." He defines himself that way, and then he moves through the world with that feeling of lack. Do you remember the lecture I mentioned in the previous chapter, about the "father without a father" conference?

YEHUDA: Yes.

ESTHER: I gave an example of a patient who had lost his father and made himself a habit of asking several people's advice whenever he intended to start a new business. Wonder of wonders, every piece of advice he receives was something along the line of, "You shouldn't," "It won't work out," etc. That's how he perpetuated his "I don't have a father" story.

YEHUDA: I think his motivation must have been to receive some compassion for not having a father, which is why he had to recreate the "no father" situation.

But it isn't a question of identity; he did it for compassion, to position himself in the "no father" stance. It isn't about identity.

ESTHER: In that case, there must be something here I'm missing.

YEHUDA: Okay. The difference is between depression as a function of structure and depression which is not a function of structure. "A function of structure" means creating a lack through one of the three previously discussed strategies: either I'm choosing the person who will deprive me, or I provoke them in order to become deprived, or I imagine I'm being deprived. The important thing is, I want to be in lack, because without lack I have no desire. If it leads to depression, it's a side effect of a strategy to experience and express a lack, a desire.

ESTHER: Okay.

YEHUDA: But in the case of the orphan, his lack does not generate desire. It isn't a strategy. But sometimes the two types of depression mix together. There are situations where the lack is created for historical or biographical reasons.

ESTHER: It doesn't create desire but it does contribute to the creation of an identity.

YEHUDA: The structural strategy exists in order to generate desire. There are situations in which the loss is not intended to create desire. When deprivation or guilt are so intense that desire is erased, that is like a computer error. The original plan was for the deprivation or the prohibition –

ESTHER: To keep the flame of desire burning.

YEHUDA: To create the desire. But normal grief – a person who lost his wife six months ago and is still grieving – is not something a person asks for; it isn't the way that –

ESTHER: It isn't his theater.

YEHUDA: It isn't his theatre, and the fact that this grief sometimes lasts thirty or forty years doesn't necessarily mean they asked for it.

ESTHER: Doesn't mean it's his theatre.

YEHUDA: Correct.

ESTHER: Meaning, he doesn't have the motivation –

YEHUDA: That's right.

ESTHER: To use the lack in order to create desire.

YEHUDA: Correct. That's why when I fight against depression I try to find out if it's the basic phenomenon or the side effect of a structure. If it's the side effect of a structure, we'll treat the structure. If not, we'll accept the loss through compassion.

ESTHER: Okay. In that case, when you use the term "identity," I understand that for you a lack that creates an identity is hysterical neurosis.

YEHUDA: Right. Right.

ESTHER: So now I understand. Identity and desire go hand in hand.

YEHUDA: Yes.

ESTHER: In theory, my identity as someone who's being deprived and my desire as someone who is lacking because of deprivation are one and the same.

YEHUDA: Right. And the key word connecting identity with desire is "subject." The subject exists by virtue of desiring. And a subject exists in the context of being recognized by an other.

ESTHER: I don't have it because I lost it, because I lost my wife six months ago – that's not an identity narrative. I don't have it because someone took it away from me – that is a narrative for the purpose of identity.

YEHUDA: Yes. In deprivation, there is a plea, a demand, a communication to an other and self-representation as a desiring subject. The widower, the fact that he's lacking – that's pure pain, not something he's asking for or inventing. And I want to finish up something I started saying earlier about psychosis: there, depression results from the fact that the subject doesn't really exist. Depression, a cutoff from life, is always lurking. That is the post-psychotic depression, which occurs when delusion can no longer give meaning to life. This is the melancholic type of depression. Unlike the neurotic depression that complains, the psychotic depression is mute.

ESTHER: Generally speaking, the loss of a symptom can generate depression, not only for a psychotic person.

YEHUDA: Anxiety or depression. Anxiety – because the symptom sustains desire with structure, with a clear target and path – a path that is continuously frustrated, but clear nonetheless. While remaining with a libido without being able to channel it through a symptom creates anxiety. Now: if exhaustion from anxiety leads to no longer wanting desire, that can cause depression. If the desire is unbearable because it is anxious, because there is no defined object; if a patient has enough of anxiety, they can unconsciously lead themselves to depression.

ESTHER: Shall we discuss an example? Earlier, I mentioned someone who had cheated on his wife. He cheated on her repeatedly, for years. This was convenient for him – he did the forbidden thing with gusto. One day, his wife had enough. She didn't want him anymore, and they broke up. This was done against his will. He wasn't interested in a separation; he was interested in infidelity, in the forbidden act. And then, suddenly, it was like "anything goes." Ever since "anything goes," his desire has decreased, because when desire is connected to the prohibition, to sin, it diminishes when the sin is no longer forbidden. Now he's at risk of depression, if I'm not mistaken.

YEHUDA: That's right.

ESTHER: I believe soon he's going to tell me that he is deeply sad that his wife left him. That all of a sudden, he realizes how much she means to him. In other words, he's going to be depressed because he lost something critical, and in a way he is right. Because his way of life was attached to a symptom, and this attachment, this "life according to a symptom," is lost.

YEHUDA: Right.

ESTHER: Now let's talk about suicide. In the text, we are reading in the Forum Lacan Tel Aviv (Lacan's Seminar 19), there is a sentence about the "absolute act" of suicide.

YEHUDA: Yes.

ESTHER: I think there's a key there to a possible approach to this act.

YEHUDA: Let me explain what an act is, and then we can understand why suicide is considered an absolute act. An "act" is something that changes the action-taker to the core. We can refer to an act as "suicidal" even if it doesn't actually entail an attempt to end one's life. When a person performs a wedding act, they become married. It's a whole other creature. They are no longer the single person they were until now. The act of getting married causes the death of the single subject, and the birth of a new person. In this way, it is similar to suicide. Lots of inhibitions people experience are related to the avoidance of the suicidal aspect of the act: in order to quit smoking, it isn't enough to give up the cigarette. One has to give up their identity as a smoker and become somebody else – a non-smoker. The clearer it is how much an act involves suicide and rebirth, the easier it is to break a habit. Giving up a habit means agreeing to a massive transformation, much greater than it seems. It isn't just getting rid of an object, but replacing the subject.

ESTHER: Or, in simpler terms, changing identities.

YEHUDA: Right. And with regards to actual suicide: sometimes people commit suicide because they are trying to generate a transformation. They have a fantasy that there is something for them on the other side. I think the healthiest approach to the issue of suicide is to acknowledge it as a choice. In working with people whose loved ones killed themselves, I have found this to be the most productive way: understanding that this was a subject's choice to end their lives, and to respect that. It means you didn't choose but they did, and it was a legitimate choice on their part.

ESTHER: There's something difficult about that. As far as I understand, what destabilizes a person who loses a loved one to suicide are question like, "Did they not love me enough? Did I not matter to them?" These are inescapable questions.

YEHUDA: You thought they loved you very much, and there's no doubt you were right about that. Don't undermine this knowledge. But understand that the pain was so great that even the most intense love could not trump it. That can help you respect their choice.

Chapter 14

Buddhist Ethics and Relativistic Ethics Meet

Before Parting

A final discussion about questions of ethics: what is the right way to live, what is the preferable way to live? How much control can one attain over their lives?

Also: how ought we treat someone who has hurt us? When is taking medication an escape and when is it pragmatic? When is there a choice and what exactly is responsibility? Buddhist ethics and relativistic ethics meet before we say goodbye.

ESTHER: We'll continue the conversation about depression in a moment. This topic, depression, raises questions of ethics that I think we ought to address, especially since we're close to the end of this book.

What I wanted us to discuss once again was the question of antidepressant medication, which have become prevalent. Since antidepressants are so common, I thought we ought to discuss them. I want to ask you what you think about this. I'll be specific, because there is one particular aspect I'm interested in. People say, "I *have* depression" as if they are saying "I have a disease," and this word choice already turns the state of mind we call "depression" into an object of essence, an object one can *have*. So someone "has" depression and takes pills, and they are effective. The scientific work in this context is certainly impressive; there is no doubt about the effectiveness of antidepressants. Under the influence of these medications, people report significant improvement. Many say, "I have the same thoughts, but they don't bring me down." The idea is that when previously depressing thoughts are no longer depressing, there's a good chance that the mind would rid itself of them and, as a byproduct, of the change they demand from the thinker. In other words, medication prevents depression and can also prevent the mental work depression demands. Does this not become a habit, in which the mind doesn't practice its own "muscles" to eradicate depression, or, worse, to understand it? Don't you think this goes against the power of the mind, any mind, to do the work itself?

YEHUDA: I think this is something to discuss in treatment. Alternatively, people can talk to themselves even when they are not in treatment and ask this question.

DOI: 10.4324/9781003342458-14

Am I listening to my depression? For example, if depression instructs me to behave differently, to make other choices, should I really ignore it? Perhaps I should change the thought patterns that lead to depression? Perhaps I should give up my narcissistic expectations, the ones that cause me to assume I deserve everything and if I don't get what I deserve I become depressed. If I've thought about it, and I'm willing to acknowledge that no one owes me a thing but I'm still depressed, and I'm doing everything I can to take care of myself – I work out, for example – everything I can think of to overcome the depression by myself and it still isn't enough – in that case, it's certainly recommended to receive medical help. It's better to feel good, no matter how. The idea that any mental phenomenon can be eradicated only by mental work is somewhat narcissistic.

ESTHER: And yet, there is still a question there. I understand your idea: "I'm checking why I'm depressed and what depression is trying to tell me." And as you added, "If nothing else works, I'll take medication." But I have doubts, because if I check what the depression is telling me, then there is a possibility to overcome it. It's always there, that's my opinion.

YEHUDA: It doesn't always work. The narcissism can work both ways. A person can be depressed because their narcissistic expectations don't materialize or because they narcissistically refuse to give up their autonomy and be helped chemically. Sometimes a person has to give up their narcissistic expectations and get over the depression by getting pharmacological help. It's certainly possible that there is something mental they cannot take care of, though they've tried. In this case, there are two options: either live well with medication or be stubborn and suffer. It's better to live well. We can't change everything, even if it's mental. It's worth a shot, but it isn't worth it to live poorly in the name of principles, which is in itself a kind of dictatorship: "You must dig through your unconscious as if you are responsible for everything and able to fix everything through the power of awareness."

ESTHER: I see this as ethics, as a question of ethics.

YEHUDA: The expectation to be able to change one's mind without outside help – whether chemical or professional – is also a kind of ego fantasy. I'm all for challenging our independence, but I'm opposed to pretension. If there is effective help, and we've made sure we've done everything we can do on our own, then it makes sense to receive every possible help. If, for instance, a twenty-two-year-old guy does his best to keep it together, to study, to work, and his parents are able to help him – and it won't make him lazy because he is doing his best – I'm all for getting help. If it doesn't corrupt, I'm all for it. So you ask if medication can corrupt a person's readiness to take care of themselves? To challenge them to live out their desires? Indeed, it can, just like financial support from one's parents can, but it won't *necessarily* corrupt them.

ESTHER: In that case, this is one aspect of the question: the ethical aspect. The second aspect has to do with the limits of a treatment's effectiveness. I'm asking about this because the question of effectiveness comes up in the context of psychoanalysis and medicinal treatment of depression. I think that, theoretically, this question is important, and I wouldn't take it lightly. A close friend of mine got cancer at the exact age that his father died of cancer many years ago. This friend was in treatment at the time of his father's death, and for years afterwards. Now, let's put aside the genetic possibility, which is a big question. Positioning the genetic possibility against the mental possibility, along with mental treatment, means positioning two paradigms against each other. These are body-mind relationship questions. Lots of what we're dealing with here with regards to depression has to do, in my opinion, with the question of the relationship between body and mind, or in accordance: materialist vs. mentalist worldview. So let's assume this isn't about genetics; there are no genetic markers – indeed, this man did not carry a cancer-related gene – and it still happened. Since he is not a carrier, one can assume there are mental reasons. Is there much point, in your opinion, to the statement that his psychoanalysis was not effective enough?

YEHUDA: Let's use an even clearer example: Freud kept smoking cigars almost till the day he died, even though it caused his cancer. The reason, as he himself explained it, was that nicotine helped him think, and if he couldn't think, he wouldn't be able to write, and wouldn't really be Freud. It was better to be Freud –

ESTHER: For a shorter time.

YEHUDA: For a shorter time, than not to be Freud at all.

ESTHER: Than to be not-Freud for a long time.

YEHUDA: That's why longevity is not the only value of life. The existence of a self-loyal subject who writes what he wants to write even at the price of shortening his life, is a choice.

ESTHER: That's a clear example of choice, of an especially great master who can say: I choose this. But I'm asking about the unconscious.

YEHUDA: You're asking if cancer can be an unconscious choice.

ESTHER: Yes, even in analysis.

YEHUDA: I suppose so. I suppose there are some situations in which a person can unconsciously choose to make far-reaching changes in their body. Should we address this with the term "control?" Supposedly, we make a conscious decision to make this choice? I don't think so. The unconscious is exactly that: unconscious. There is a limit to our responsibility for our unconscious choices.

ESTHER: What you just said is that, indeed, there is a mental action. Or: there could be an unconscious mental decision to contract a serious illness. I'll phrase what you said as I understand it: If we're dealing with the relationship of body and mind, what you said is that the mind can certainly influence massive processes in the body.

YEHUDA: I believe so. There is no proof.

ESTHER: Excellent. The humility seems appropriate, but this statement is important.

YEHUDA: But at the same time, we must remember: there are some events that are not mental. Some things are not psychology. There's genetics, there's chemistry, and there's physiology. The sheep in Australia who have skin cancer because of the hole in the ozone layer – I don't think there's an emotional component to that. And I think quite a few people who have skin cancer have it not because of an emotional component. Where exactly is the line? To what extent are things given to our choice and our control? I think we ought to approach this pragmatically. Would it help to think so? Is there anything we can do about it? All right, let's assume it's mental. What are you going to do? If the illness is a reminder that we ought to change our lifestyle, then we ought to. That doesn't mean that is the reason for the disease or the cure for it, but it's certainly an opportunity to do your best for your own good.

ESTHER: So, ultimately, your final ethical stance is a pragmatic one.

YEHUDA: Yes, when it concerns what we don't know.

ESTHER: You said two things today. You said: we don't know, but we might assume that the mind has a great influence over the body. And second: the principle according to which we should handle the body-mind question is a pragmatic one.

YEHUDA: The question is, do I define the problem as grandiosity or as avoiding responsibility. If I say, "I'm not doing enough, I need to dig deeper," it's a sign I'm afraid of shirking responsibility. If I think every mark on my skin is my responsibility, I'm suffering of an excess of control, a grandiosity that causes me to collapse under the weight of the guilt. So, what hurts worse right now? Being guilty because you control everything, or being helpless because you can control nothing? What is the balancing point that suits you right now? There are some therapeutic cases – for instance, a mother who feels guilty for her child's autism – in which the unequivocal goal is to snap out of the grandiose narcissism related to the assumption that everything is up to her. She has to accept that some things have no reason, are not your fault or your responsibility, not under your control. There are conflicting situations, like when someone is running late because of traffic. They chose to leave home when traffic was heavy. Where is their personal responsibility? When is it right to challenge their responsibility and when is it better to challenge their acknowledgement of their own helplessness? We each need to find our own balance point for every issue. But it's also important to pick a side. Otherwise, you may stay in a situation where you're both guilty and helpless. If you think you're guilty, make a change. If you can't, you're helpless. Accept it. Loosen your grip.

ESTHER: Okay, we'll get into that dilemma in a minute; a dilemma about the ethics of choice. I want to introduce another aspect of the body-mind dialectics and the way our culture is confused about it. I want to argue that we are confused about it, to a great extent, because of psychological, and particularly psychoanalytic thought. Psychoanalytic thought, the one that deals with the relationship between early childhood and the shaping of our inner world, the shaping of a subject, constitutes a dominant factor in our culture. Freud introduced a way of thinking that acts as a companion to materialistic thought. They each do its job, but when they come together, problematic cultural phenomena come up. I'll explain this in a moment. Let's start with the fact that there is no moral thought. You aren't talking about morals anymore either; you're talking about responsibility. But I think the two are connected.

Let me tell you a short story. One day, I heard a news story about a murder trial in the United States. The defense line was scientific: the defendant was diagnosed as a psychopath. Then, to our amazement, we found out that, much like any other human phenomenon, psychopathy is genetic! This was the line of defense, supported by an expert. I call this scientific materialism. Since this was proven, the man could plead not guilty, by reason of genetics. And something else was also proved. Let's assume that "proved" signifies something we believe in a scientific-reliant civilization. We're talking about scientific proof and advance through life while relying on science. It was proven, then, that if someone "has" a psychopathic gene, and in addition was treated poorly by their mother in childhood, there's a good chance that this gene will take behavioral effect, actualized in this person's adult life. So here was a murderer whose mother treated him poorly – she was violent – and he has a gene. You put two and two together, and the man is declared by the court not to be responsible for his actions. In other words, the combination of psychoanalytic thought, which argues a causal relationship between childhood and adulthood, along with materialistic scientific thought (in this case, a psychopathic gene), clearly changes the legal interpretation – and the murderer's sentence! Long story short, if you bring a doctor's note to court, you'll be exonerated. What I'm telling you is the court accepted this claim and the sentence was significantly mitigated. That's why I'm arguing that the combination of a materialistic culture and psychoanalytic thought creates an individual that is no longer a subject in terms of choice. It isn't clear that anything can be chosen anymore, if you have a mean mother and you carry some gene or another.

YEHUDA: The great service Freud did for humankind by coining the term "unconscious," was that he defined it as an area devoid of guilt but still containing responsibility. Meaning, it was not your choice to have your mother treat you the way she did. That isn't your fault, and yet you do have a responsibility. As soon as you realize this influence on you, you have the choice not to be subjected to it. As soon as you are aware –

ESTHER: But you "have the gene," so how can you?

YEHUDA: I'm not talking about the gene. I've got no recourse for the gene. The question is, what can I do with the "mother's fault" interpretation, which is almost like a gene itself.

ESTHER: Yes: no less deterministic.

YEHUDA: So I'm saying, something can be done. You didn't choose the hand you were dealt, including the way your mother treated you. But as soon as you're aware of the influence of what happened to you in childhood, you've got responsibility. If a person takes medication that makes them fall asleep at the wheel, and they are not aware of this side effect, then it isn't their fault, nor their responsibility. But as soon as they know, they can be careful, meaning, assume responsibility. If someone spills coffee on the table, it's their fault. But if I want the table to be clean, it's my responsibility to clean it. That's why I pin responsibility to a person aware of their influences they were subjected to, and their ability to resist them. They can resist them only when they are aware of them. There are situations in which, even though they are aware, they cannot resist. If they can't, they bear no responsibility. Who defines whether or not they can? The person themselves. I'm not a legal scholar. I, as a psychoanalyst, ask the person what they are guilty of and responsible for. That same psychopath, had he come to treatment agonized with guilt, then by definition he wouldn't be a psychopath.

ESTHER: Right.

YEHUDA: That's why, as far as I'm concerned, he isn't guilty, because he isn't undergoing treatment to acknowledge his guilt.

ESTHER: So the only responsible people are those who acknowledge responsibility.

YEHUDA: As a judge, I would search for balance; whatever is best for society. That's the judge's job. In a society where everyone is a licensed psychopath, their license still ought to be revoked. In a society where people are expected to assume responsibility for their genetics – I'm intentionally exaggerating – we ought to lighten the load of responsibility a bit. So it's a question of balance. When would I take the psychoanalytic angle? When a person wants to forgive. Then they ask themselves: Did the person who hurt me do so out of choice? Another option is to think of the offending party as the corner of a table that I hurt my shin on; someone activated by their genes. The question is, do you want them in your life as a subject. If you do, you must lay blame on them and demand that they take responsibility. The determining factor is whether I treat the other as subject or object, as a person responsible for their choices or as an object shifted upon a board. What role do I offer them in my life? I can treat them like a baby whom I don't expect to be responsible for their choices, or like a friend, whose promises I count on and who is responsible to keep them. Do I expect responsibility from this person, or not? It depends what role I want them to have in my life – that of a subject or that of an object.

ESTHER: It's practically absolute relativism!

YEHUDA: Yes.

ESTHER: It's functional morality.

YEHUDA: More than that, it's narrative: what story do I want to tell? What view of reality do I choose? It's a postmodern position.

ESTHER: That's what I'm saying, yes. It's a position in which the moral perception doesn't rely on an absolute value but is at the service of the subject, innate to the subject rather than exterior. In other words, non-transcendental . . .

YEHUDA: Indeed. When the principle we hold onto is not reality, pleasure takes on the status of principle: what is the worldview that allows desire and *jouissance*? Too much guilt? Too little responsibility? What is the plot a person tells, the one in which they live, and which sustains them as subjects, as desiring, as enjoying? One could, if one so chooses, void the plot of any narrative quality and live a dry life in the sense that any sexual desire is referred to as "hormones" and any murderous desire as "psychopathy."

ESTHER: Or "psychopathic genetics."

YEHUDA: One could void life of its meaning of drives and lead it to lack all satisfaction. That is a person's choice, how dry and technical to make their life, how cynical, or, on the contrary, to take responsibility and give life meaning.

ESTHER: Hang on –

YEHUDA: And there is such a thing – excess meaning, as well as lack of meaning.

ESTHER: I'd like to linger on one point of what you said, which I'm interested in because I perceive it as opposed to Buddhist ethics. You say this: if you want this person, who failed, who insulted – the person who hurt you, all right? I'm looking for a non-moral descriptor – if you want this person in your life, you must treat them as a subject, as someone who bears responsibility for their actions, right? Only that way can they participate in your life.

YEHUDA: Correct. "If you want to remain my friend, you must agree to accept my anger, because otherwise I'm going to write you off. Moreover, I'd have nobody to be angry at, because you won't be a subject anymore."

ESTHER: Right. Listen to this interesting idea: the starting point of Buddhist thought is a dialectic of wisdom and ignorance. That's the fundamental choice. In this sense, it resembles psychoanalytic thought. In truth, it's an ethics, because you cannot prove it, but it has an a-priori moral stance: it's better to know than not to know. I'm not at all sure you agree with me that this is the psychoanalytic ethics. But in Buddhism, the choice is: to know or not to know. Using the human's ability to know who they are in order to become fully human, to actualize your humanity: being a creature of choice. I'm saying this with regards to what you said before: "I can only attribute responsibility to someone who knows."

YEHUDA: Indeed, and Freud viewed a refusal to know as an objection to be overcome, while Lacan respected the right not to know and placed the objection on the clinician's side.

ESTHER: While Buddhism says: and everyone else is ignorant. Ignorance is a human option. Not knowing one's own intentions, not knowing what leads one to do what they do, not taking responsibility for the outcomes – that is all ignorance. Those who practice Buddhism take full responsibility for the world. Those who accept the Law of Karma – which states that anything you do, big or small, has a deep effect on the world – choose knowledge and wisdom. As such, they are aware of the fact that many have not chosen the path of wisdom and do not understand the motives and outcomes of their actions. They are, therefore, ignorant. Evil is attributed to ignorance, as is excessive desire. They are born of ignorance. And there is no room for anger when addressing ignorance.

YEHUDA: It sounds like those who are enlightened, those who are not ignorant, forgive everyone else because they don't believe everyone else has a choice. Am I getting this right?

ESTHER: Not entirely. They believe others have choice but don't know it. They think every person has a choice. That's critical.

YEHUDA: Ignorance is lack of awareness of choice. Is that right? If you attribute to someone a lack of responsibility for their choices on the basis of ignorance, of course you cannot be angry with them.

ESTHER: They aren't angry with anyone. The division you stated – into subjects and non-subjects – does not exist. A wrong action is always the result of ignorance, and those who perform it are in a state of ignorance and therefore there is no reason to be angry with them.

YEHUDA: The Buddhist axiom is that human nature is fundamentally good, and anyone acting differently is ignorant. They are not familiar with their own true, good nature.

ESTHER: There is an original nature which is clear, and there are the roots of suffering, which are also part of human nature, and the first and deepest root is ignorance. It can be uprooted, or not.

YEHUDA: Freud assumes that human nature is fundamentally aggressive: if you want to take down the primordial father, the only way to do so is to come together and murder him, as in the fable of *Totem and Taboo*. When Einstein asked him what to do with the cruel, fascist, indulgent father (Hitler, Mussolini, etc., this conversation took place between the two world wars), Freud answered: only violence can handle violence. We must come together and fight. We cannot expect justice to happen on its own. Meaning, human nature is aggressive and we ought to use force for our own survival.

ESTHER: For our theoretical purposes: Buddhism does not argue that human nature is good from childhood, as opposed to the biblical quote about the human heart being evil from childhood. Buddhism states the two choices that people have available to them. There is no discussion of good and evil as absolute values; there is a discussion of inner ethics, and inner ethics is subject to individual choice.

YEHUDA: And here is the Lacanian ethics of guilt: the only thing a person can be guilty of is not acting according to their own desire. Meaning, it isn't morality in the sense of a duty toward humankind. The moral obligation is to be attentive to one's desire. Since desire takes place in the subject and the subject is a social creature – contextual as a word in a sentence – attentiveness to desire goes hand in hand with social belonging and acting for the good of a person's sustaining environment. It, therefore, follows that, according to Lacan, the subject is fundamentally good.

Chapter 15

At Last – Love

I want to know what love is. I want you to show me.

– Birds chirp outside our window –

ESTHER: What should we talk about this morning? Love?

YEHUDA: Death? Or love? Love is more complicated than death, so let's –

ESTHER: So let's go for it!

YEHUDA: All right.

ESTHER: Love is more complicated, huh?

YEHUDA: I think . . . it's complicated to say anything about it.

ESTHER: Complicated is good. Okay.

YEHUDA: The well-known side of love is that it constitutes part of the story, a love story, a love letter – something that exists in a text, something that exists in people's conversations, and therefore something learned, just like the entire range of emotions is something learned, because not all emotions exist in every culture. One of Lacan's statements was that "there is no sexual relation," meaning there is no complete satisfaction, complete suitability, complete compatibility, no complete fulfilment of all wishes. It comes from the fact that love takes place in the story, and there is no complete suitability between the real world and the story.

ESTHER: What you just said, quoting Lacan's ideas about the lack of sexual relation, is that there is no subject in the world that can fully fulfil the wishes of another subject. "There is no sexual relation" means there is no person in the world who perfectly suits another, who perfectly fills the other's lacks. That's very important. That, in my opinion, is the root of the pain people cause each other. Many assume that a romantic relationship is founded on a mutual commitment to fulfil the wishes of their partners. "I need him to be strong. He promised to be strong for me! But I discovered he isn't really strong." Then it's very difficult to accept the partners' imperfection in terms of their ability to fill my lacks. That's why, for the purpose of this book, "there is no sexual relation" is critical.

YEHUDA: Indeed.

DOI: 10.4324/9781003342458-15

ESTHER: The bitter disappointment people experience in a prolonged romantic relationship results from the fact that the other subject – the partner – supposedly promised me they would be what I need them to be, then didn't keep their promise. That is the bitter, exacting calculation partners on the verge of breakup make.

YEHUDA: Right. And the beloved – what role can they have in relation to the unfulfilled wish? A comforting one. Love is a type of comfort or compensation, sharing the sorrow for the fact that wishes can never be fully fulfilled by the other. Meaning, they can share that idea of "no sexual relation."

ESTHER: Meaning, feeling sorry for your beloved for the fact that you've let them down, acknowledge it and don't get hurt. Yes.

YEHUDA: Let's say that's what we can do in couple's therapy. Couples who come to therapy because they are disappointed in each other can eventually come to the point of comforting each other for the fact that wishes don't always come true. But the next step would be to recognize that one's partner isn't even supposed to make these wishes come true. So there is no room for demanding or anger. A separation founded in anger is not yet ripe. Only when the person ending the relationship says, "You owe me nothing and I have no complaints, but I'm disappointed and believe I can be happier," are they truly ready to break up. They are choosing it out of full personal responsibility. I encountered a case in which the person who ended the relationship did so because their partner was demanding fulfilment from them. They fled from the demanding partner, who continued to complain and make demands even after they broke up, as if the separation wasn't legitimate, either. Sometimes seeing the breakup as legitimate is the very thing that creates a possibility to live happily together, without anger or demands. There are times when separation is the only way to establish separateness – meaning, the fact that there are no dues. From the moment the separateness is established, there are no more demands, no more anger, and no reason to break up. The separation acts as a kind of relationship reboot.

ESTHER: Something interesting just happened: we said we would talk about love and it was obvious to both of us that we meant romantic love.

YEHUDA: Indeed.

ESTHER: So, we're talking about "love" in general, we agreed that would be the subject of the penultimate chapter of our book, and it's an enormous topic, but somehow it was clear to both of us that we were talking about a couple's love, sexual love. We didn't consider the fact that the very same word is used to describe other kinds of love: the love of a child for a parent, of a parent for a child, and more and more. I think this happened because we live in a culture in which romantic love is put on a pedestal. Am I wrong?

YEHUDA: Let's start at the beginning. Love has an aspect of drive before it even becomes a story. Before love splits in a child's soul into emotional love and sexual love, in the beginning of love, they are united. What a child feels for their mother is an indiscriminate attraction. The prohibition on incest causes them to split those emotions. That's why, before the split, a drive-based, sexual element surely exists. You're saying there is familial love and friendly love and romantic love – all sorts of love, within which romantic love is distinguished through sexuality – but in the beginning, sexuality is a part of every kind of love. So, to address cultural characteristics, perhaps what characterizes our culture, which distinguishes between romantic love and other loves and puts the emphasis on romantic love –

ESTHER: That's the aspiration for a pre-Oedipal state, that's what you're saying.

YEHUDA: Yes. Romantic love ensures that. Romantic love promises the lost wholeness and fullness, the one that once was, before the child was forbidden from experiencing it.

ESTHER: I never thought about it that way: at first there was unity. Originally, love was whole rather than split.

YEHUDA: A common phenomenon that Freud discussed with regards to men but can also be witnessed in women, is that they have trouble attributing a romantic object and a sexual object to the same person. That's one dominant reason for a lack of loyalty in relationships.

ESTHER: Yes.

YEHUDA: People have all sorts of solutions: they have one partner for some needs and another partner for other needs, or different ways of treating the same partner – couples in which there are different relationships between partners, as if they were two separate couples within sexuality and outside of it. There is a structural contradiction between love and sexuality: sexuality is the more drive-based aspect, more selfish, more objectifying – reminiscent of one's relationship to food. A person wants to take pleasure in food and be satiated. Sometimes, in sexuality, the other doesn't necessarily have to be there . . .

ESTHER: The "other" in what sense?

YEHUDA: The partner. The sexual partner doesn't have to be a subject, doesn't have to be human, doesn't have to be part of a non-selfish relationship. But we are used to thinking of love as a form of giving – for instance, when it comes to children – while here, in a romantic relationship that is meant to sustain love and sexuality simultaneously, there is a contradiction between the sexuality that has an aspect of "taking" and between love, whose central aspect is "giving." The frame that can contain both of them, and is a sort of sharing of the idea of "no sexual relation," is intimacy. Intimacy is the readiness to play a role in the sexual fantasy of the other. "I allow you to be selfish toward me and in my presence, therefore I love you." That's intimacy – legitimizing drives and making room for them.

ESTHER: But that is the gift of love and there is no need for another definition: someone gives something to someone else. Someone is willing to be something that isn't them for someone else.

YEHUDA: Correct.

ESTHER: They are willing to be an object, somebody else's object, being what the other person asks them to be.

YEHUDA: Right, but at that moment, the other is in a selfish state. Intimacy is the love on the part of the person taking the other's devotion. It is the willingness to reveal oneself as selfish, exposed in their drives.

ESTHER: That's love. And what's on the selfish side? The side that wants to receive? That's the child. But a child loves their mother back, right? What you're saying now is that love belongs to the side that is willing to give what they don't exactly have, what isn't exactly them, what they don't want but are willing to give, and sexuality is the side that wants to receive, the side that wants –

YEHUDA: Right.

ESTHER: That wants to use the other for the fulfilment of a fantasy.

YEHUDA: Exactly.

ESTHER: That's the division you made.

YEHUDA: Yes. And now let's bring up another subject: it isn't that obvious, agreeing to be loved. We don't usually stop to think about that. If you ask people whether or not they want to be loved, most of them will say "of course." But when a person agrees to be loved, they must agree to see their partner with, I'd say, their wounds, their inferiority, their dependency. And the question is whether it's possible, for the loved one, not to detest their lover for being so exposed with their dependency. That's why people might have a difficult time being loved. On the one hand, because they despise their lover, and on the other hand because they must fulfill and satisfy and meet the expectations of their lover. Both of these things together can deter people from being loved.

ESTHER: And why would it inspire contempt? Why does seeing another in a state Freud described as "A person in love is humble"[1] inspire contempt? Does self-regard reveal someone to be pathetic? Why, really?

YEHUDA: Because there is a narcissistic fantasy of perfection, the perfection of being someone who lacks nothing and depends on no one.

ESTHER: And you see the other with their enormous lack, their inability to be within narcissistic perfection . . .

YEHUDA: That's right, exactly. In the face of a fantasy of perfection, the lover, who lack for something, seems pathetic. If the beloved is not preoccupied with their own fantasy of perfection but is in touch with their own lack and does not presume to be whole, they will not despise the lover. They will be in solidarity with the lover. They will say: yes, I know what that's like. Maybe they can return the love and maybe they can't, but they won't despise the lover's position. Often, the lover sinks into desperate insecurity. This doesn't necessarily happen because they receive a hint of rejection from their beloved. It's simply an inseparable part of being in the vulnerable lover's position.

ESTHER: Let's take this another step further, because this is really the thing. It seems like first world problems, but actually . . .

YEHUDA: Actually, they aren't. This is, in fact, a fundamental problem parents have when they refuse to be loved by their children. It isn't trivial, being loved. For lots of people it is trivial – being loved by one's child is a joy and no problem – but for some people it's difficult, just like romantic love is difficult for them, so they flee from it. It makes them anxious.

ESTHER: Why anxious?

YEHUDA: Because they have to deliver.

ESTHER: That's another story.

YEHUDA: Yes. Or it reminds them of their own lack. Lots of times the lover is charmed by a loved one that appears whole –

ESTHER: That's what I wanted to talk about. That's another problem.

YEHUDA: And when that loved one, who appears whole, returns their love – it turns out they aren't whole.

ESTHER: Right.

YEHUDA: Or else they wouldn't love them back.

ESTHER: Exactly.

YEHUDA: And then, when they love and are therefore not whole, the lover no longer loves them. There are so many "I love them as long as they don't love me back" dynamics, and that is one explanation for them.

ESTHER: Wait! I wanted to talk about the dimension of delusion that exists not in every love, but in the kind of love we refer to as "falling in love."

YEHUDA: Okay.

ESTHER: But what actually happens is humble because they see the other as whole. Now, the other, if they are willing to join this delusion, are willing to see themselves as whole, and whatever happens next happens next, right? The bubble will burst, that's part of the problem. But maybe the difficulty of being loved is just that, and that's why people become people-pleasers, because they must fulfil the wishes of the person who is in love with them, knowing they don't love you for who you are. You know this unconsciously, that they love you because they are projecting something onto you –

YEHUDA: Right, because they attribute a wholeness to you –

ESTHER: Attribute something to you that's bigger than you are, precisely.

YEHUDA: A wholeness that isn't you. And now you either meet their expectations and be whole and stop being you –

ESTHER: Yes, or you have to –

YEHUDA: Confess to being un-whole –

ESTHER: That won't help.

YEHUDA: And risk losing the love. What can help is loving, because then it's clear you are un-whole. The question is, whether or not you will continue to be loved –

ESTHER: Yes, whether the partner can take it. That's all in the Imaginary order. The danger here –

YEHUDA: The danger comes from the Imaginary.

ESTHER: That's it.

YEHUDA: Right.

ESTHER: The danger of love is in the Imaginary.

YEHUDA: Right. Now, at the same time, the Imaginary is vital to love. Without falling in love and becoming infatuated, without the experience of harmony and perfection, love would not ignite in the first place. So the question is, how do we survive the sobering. When the infatuation for the wholeness is undermined and sobering takes place, did the relationship manage to evolve in the meantime? If infatuation lasts a few months, that is the time available to develop the relationship and form love. It's a kind of grace period that allows something to happen.

ESTHER: That's interesting. For a moment I thought about the first chapter of this book and the position of orphanhood, which is the parallel of the process you're talking about now. Because a child goes through a process of sobering with their parents, in which they discover that their parents are un-whole and therefore cannot be an authority.

YEHUDA: Indeed.

ESTHER: Because the parent can't – they don't really have the tools to be an authority. And then the child – especially in adolescence, but in fact long before that – has to go through this sobering and develop solidarity with their parent. Right?

YEHUDA: Yes.

ESTHER: So we are destined – I'm generalizing here – destined to go through delusion and sobering, delusion and sobering, all throughout our lives?

YEHUDA: Right.

ESTHER: In every context.

YEHUDA: Yes. And we must take care not to refuse the delusion, because life is nothing without it. But we must also take care not to get caught up in it, because that is the source of all pain.

ESTHER: How can we do both these things?

YEHUDA: Knowing we live in a myth is no reason to refuse it, since the only alternative is the reality of myth-free trauma.

ESTHER: On the one hand, to agree to remain in the delusion, and on the other hand not to get trapped within it? I'm asking this because there are four vows a Zen Buddhist monk recites daily, and because the subject of ignorance, which is almost like a synonym for delusion, is very central to Buddhist thought; it is the starting point of suffering.

YEHUDA: Yes?

ESTHER: The first vow is: Sentient beings are infinite; we vow to save them all. The second is: Delusions are infinite, we vow to cut through them all. We'll ignore the other two vows for the moment.

YEHUDA: So where is the ignorance?

ESTHER: "Delusions are infinite."

YEHUDA: But if the goal is to reach their end, then the goal is to resist ignorance.

ESTHER: Correct.

YEHUDA: Things are different with Lacan.

ESTHER: Exactly.

YEHUDA: Okay.

ESTHER: Exactly. But pay attention to the first vow. The fact that it's the first one is meaningful. To help all beings. The second vow says, delusions are infinite and our obligation is to cut through them all. But the framework, the first vow, is compassion for all beings. Meaning, to cut through all delusions, what protects you is the knowledge that "there is no sexual relation." You first vow to love, and only later, under the condition of love, to cut through delusions. The framework of this act is one of love. It's called compassion, which is a form of love, a love that notices the other's lack.

YEHUDA: Okay.

ESTHER: You understand? A sober love.

YEHUDA: I can translate this into pragmatic ideas. What to do with suffering, how this is relevant to overcoming suffering. So –

ESTHER: If there are no delusions, there is no suffering.

YEHUDA: But if there are no delusions there is no infatuation.

ESTHER: There is love, but no infatuation.

YEHUDA: And infatuation –

ESTHER: There is no enchantment.

YEHUDA: But that's the thing – enchantment is part of life, and there is no ethics that instructs objecting to it, which might be the ethics of Buddhism. That's why, if a patient wants to know why they are in love, it's best not to answer that, because –

ESTHER: Because you'll take it apart. Because they will take it apart.

YEHUDA: Dissecting a frog to find out how it hops prevents it from ever hopping again. Infatuation is founded in ignorance. It cannot survive in the light of day. And there is no reason to turn on the light and shoo the enchantment of infatuation away, either.

ESTHER: Unless it entails too much suffering.

YEHUDA: Suffering occurs when there is abandonment. Then the patient would realize that he is still in painful love with someone a full year after she left him and come in for help getting over it. Now it's time to take apart the infatuation, from the pragmatic reason that it causes suffering. As long as it brought joy, there was no reason to take it apart. There was even hope that it was a kind of grace period that could allow the relationship to start up again.

ESTHER: Redemption, a time of redemption.

YEHUDA: Yes. But now that you're bleeding with the pain of abandonment, it's time to sober up from the delusions of what you've attributed to the loved one. What you attributed to them is the imaginary aspect of the whole beloved, the one whose love proves that you're whole, too. If heartbreak is disappointment for losing the audience who viewed me as whole, then the goal is now to separate from wholeness, and then you won't feel the need to cry for the loss of the marveling audience anymore.

But beyond the Imaginary, one thing we should not aspire to lose, and is part of love, even unrequited love, is that when someone loves me, I love them for recognizing my desire. This takes place in treatment, too: when you fall in love with your psychoanalyst, you fall in love with the person who helps you find out your unconscious desires, the one making your desires accessible to you so you can try to make them come true. When someone does that kind of thing for me, I love them for it. It's gratitude for bringing me closer to myself.

ESTHER: That's a critical function of love. It's very important.

YEHUDA: It's the function of love as it appears in treatment, in psychoanalysis.

ESTHER: But not only.

YEHUDA: True.

ESTHER: Not only at all.

YEHUDA: Right. And that's why, if we ask about this function, how it's relevant to getting over unrequited love, I'd ask the abandoned lover what desire was recognized in them through this relationship.

ESTHER: Yehuda, you need to explain that, this idea of loving the person who recognizes your desires. I don't think it's clear enough. What does it mean "loving them for recognizing your desires?" Do you mean the desires one is too embarrassed to recognize or can't recognize?

YEHUDA: Exactly. For instance, if a patient loves somebody, or something, and is not in touch with these desires, they appear along with a resistance, along with contempt for people who love these things. I'm intentionally avoiding giving a specific example, so that each person can recognize themselves in this situation. If the clinician says, "Here's your desire," based on a slip of the tongue, or a dream, or a recurring theme, based on something the patient said without even noticing it – they are giving it back to the patient, telling them what they see – the patient's desire. And the patient, who resists this at first, because they were embarrassed by this thing originally, then has second thoughts and experiences a connection to themselves. They say, "Now I know who I am. I've been looking for myself for years and finally found myself, thanks to this person who pointed out my true desires. I feel like hugging them, this person who brought me closer to myself." In romantic love, we attribute this ability to our beloved.

ESTHER: Yes. This man told me I'd look great in high heels. I hate high heels and despise women who wear them, but he said it, so I tried them on and realized I look stunning.

YEHUDA: Right.

ESTHER: And that wearing high heels excites me.

YEHUDA: Yes. Yes.

ESTHER: Or making money, starting a successful business, you can do it, sure you can.

YEHUDA: Right, right.

ESTHER: And then it turns out you really can.

YEHUDA: Yes, but there are two layers here: if I love him for recognizing my talents and ability and how good I look in high heels and all that, it's still narcissistic. It's still recognizing my wholeness.

ESTHER: Yes.

YEHUDA: I'm talking about what's beyond that, when a person recognizes my desire. When they don't tell me I look good in heels, but rather, "I recognize that you like heels."

ESTHER: Okay, they point at my desire, not at the fact that I'm wonderful in some way or another.

YEHUDA: I once knew a woman who fell in love with her standup teacher. She wanted to be a standup artist. When that love became unrequited, the first level was, "He recognized your talent, and now that he's gone you might feel as if you are untalented, which is part of heartbreak. Now let's see if you can stop needing him, just look at the audience and hear the applause and realize you are talented without him telling you that." If this process is successful, then –

ESTHER: Then we gain something.

YEHUDA: Then the beloved becomes redundant, which is vital in the case of a love that comes to an end. But let's go deeper: this man didn't only recognize how funny she was. He recognized how much she loved to make people laugh. That's the essential thing. Now she must hold onto her desire without others having to point it out. It's very useful to have others point it out. It enables us to recognize it and sustain it. But then do we really depend on the other, or have they already done their job by recognizing and getting us to acknowledge our desire, and now we can move on? That's why treatment can come to an end, too. The clinician does the work of recognizing our desire, and at the end of treatment they are no longer essential. The desire is recognized and is now at the service of the subject. Things are different in love life: we don't seek out the breakup, but if we experience it, against our will, we can accept it the way we end treatment. We can take ownership of our desire.

ESTHER: Okay.

YEHUDA: Taking ownership of my desire, so that I no longer depend on the person who recognized it. But that isn't a goal in and of itself, it's just a way to get over a breakup, to break free of my dependence on the person who recognized my desire. That is the goal for treatment, but not for life. I have no reason to break free from the person who helps me recognize my desire. But if, against my will, I lose them, then I'd better learn to live without them. But the independence in recognizing my desire – that is not a goal. People depend on each other, and that's just fine.

ESTHER: For that purpose. People depend on each other for that.

YEHUDA: Yes.

ESTHER: Is that, then, the essence of dependence?

YEHUDA: Dependence has many forms. But, specifically, dependence on a person who recognizes my desires for me is not a bad thing. The idea that it's something we ought to overcome, and depend on nobody to recognize our desires is a narcissistic idea of autonomy, of "I don't need anybody." That's why I'm qualifying this statement and saying that breaking free of my dependence on the person who recognizes my desires is only essential if this dependence doesn't work. In treatment, dependence develops for the need for self-discovery, for breaking free of all sorts of fantasies and inhibitions – there, breaking free from dependence is essential, and then treatment comes to an end.

ESTHER: We're actually talking about a factor that is crucial for love, when we're talking about being in love with the person who recognizes your desires.

YEHUDA: Yes.

ESTHER: We're talking about something essential.

YEHUDA: Yes, someone who knows me. Who knows me deeply.

ESTHER: That's what people mean when they say, "this person knows me."

YEHUDA: Yes. That's the person who knows me. Because who's "me?" What's this "me" that the other person knows? It's the thing I identify with, the I. I identify with my shape, with my last name, and according to Lacanian ethics, the ultimate thing to identify with is my desire. That's why I am grateful to the person who recognizes my desire, and this gratitude is called love.

Note

1 Freud, S. (2001 [1914]) *On Narcissism: An Introduction.* In The standard edition (Vol. 14). London: Vintage.

Reference

Freud, S. (2001[1914]) *On Narcissism: An Introduction.* In The standard edition (Vol. 14). London: Vintage.

Chapter 16

And Finally

Death

ESTHER: Good morning, Yehuda.

YEHUDA: Good morning, Esther.

ESTHER: This chapter is going to be the last one in our book.

YEHUDA: Indeed.

ESTHER: And it's no coincidence that we decided the final chapter of this book would deal with death, because we believe discussing death doesn't have to be depressing, right?

YEHUDA: Very true.

ESTHER: Otherwise, we wouldn't agree to have this be the last chapter of our book, because we have no desire to depress people who have made the effort of reading and understanding this far.

YEHUDA: On the contrary.

ESTHER: That's why we must discuss death as a fact about which, just like many other facts of life, we must find an effective stance.

YEHUDA: Excellent.

ESTHER: And how are we going to do that?

YEHUDA: First, we have no clue, absolutely no clue, about death. People in general don't. We have all sorts of imaginary ideas about death. One of the most common metaphors about the experience of death is that it's an experience of rejection or ostracizing, of exclusion, while those are the social experiences of a living person who feels left out. We often use this idea of being ostracized to talk about being dead. I can say from my personal experience that when I was close to death, I had dreams of social exclusion. This is the form my unconscious gave –

ESTHER: To death.

YEHUDA: It's like not being invited to a party. The party is over for you, it keeps going without you. This is just a metaphor, because in truth we have no idea whether or not an awareness of what one is missing out on exists after death. That's why we'll start with the idea that every fear of death we have is based on metaphors we've assigned to it. The point is, we can be less afraid. And another thing: this experience, fear of death, can be thought of as a reminder that life is precious. The fear of death is a fear of dying before I've had a

DOI: 10.4324/9781003342458-16

chance to do what I want. So, whenever the fear arises, the question ought to come up as well – how do you need to live in order to not be afraid to die, not be afraid of missing out, of the feeling that you haven't had a chance to live yet.

ESTHER: Is there such a thing, living without the feeling of missing out?

YEHUDA: Yes. At each moment I can ask myself if I'm making choices and paying prices according to my true preferences, and if the answer is no, I can make a change and make choices for prices that match my preferences. Those who imagine that a choice comes at no price will experience a sense of missing out either way.

ESTHER: Those who imagine their choice won't have a price . . .

YEHUDA: Yes. Those who don't factor the price into their choice can feel like they've missed out. They'll feel deprived: why do they have to give up something? But those who understand clearly that every choice has a price can make a conscious decision – if the current deal doesn't sit well with them, they can change it and choose a different price for a different choice.

ESTHER: I thought we might look at another aspect, bring another theoretical element into this discussion – the subject of a death wish.

YEHUDA: The death drive.

ESTHER: That's a prevalent subject in all sorts of psychoanalytic thought.

YEHUDA: Yes.

ESTHER: From Freud onwards. The term has different interpretations, and moreover – if we don't know what death is, where does the death drive come from?

YEHUDA: The death drive is an aspiration for rest. Extreme rest. As part of our illusion that we know anything about death, we can treat death as a state of rest and relaxation, as being exempt from any effort, from being the one missing something and forced to pursue things. It's an ambition to become an object, to fully devote oneself without a will of one's own. The death drive treats the state of being dead as fulfilling the wish for extreme rest. Rest from the burden of lack, from the burden of the need to fill what is lacking, and instead to be in a state of wanting for nothing, being fully tranquil and without tension. But again, this all takes place as part of a fantasy in which we can guess what it's like to die, so we envision it like a deep rest.

ESTHER: This implies that there isn't any difference between a fantasy of wholeness and a fantasy of death.

YEHUDA: Right.

ESTHER: So, you would say that extreme narcissism contains a dimension of death drive.

YEHUDA: Correct. In extreme narcissism there is no price. It's a privileged position in which everyone owes me and must do things for me.

ESTHER: A position of a god, of a god as well, yes.

YEHUDA: If there is no lack or effort to bear, I must be striving to be dead. But again, this is all just part of a fantasy that death means extreme rest and being unburdened. It's true, the narcissist exempts themselves from the burden and puts others in the position of having to do it for him. They needn't make any effort.

ESTHER: So, a death drive and narcissism are the same thing?

YEHUDA: These are situations that are similar in that they represent a form of wholeness, images of wholeness. It can be rest, a full rest that is unlike life, in which something is always lacking and being sought out. Or in which we seek to rid ourselves of something. In subject–object relationships, this is a sado-masochistic relationship, because being in the masochistic position means being the object, and that's another way of being without initiative or lack or desire; being merely the other's object of pleasure. There's a measure of pretense in that, because the masochist is the one who initiated and invented the entire game. The idea that death is full rest also contains a measure of pretense. It's a similar game. Another situation of exemption from lack is narcissism, so whether it's masochism or narcissism or extreme devotion –

ESTHER: These are all solutions for the same problem.

YEHUDA: Indeed, solutions for the same problem. Our problem is that we lack some-thing, and these are situations in which we avoid being creatures who lack.

ESTHER: That's it.

YEHUDA: Yes, being someone who lacks means being alive. Many times, during treatment of depression, the patient grows angry. They come back to life! All of a sudden, they lack something and they become angry about this lack.

ESTHER: Meaning, depression contains a death drive?

YEHUDA: Yes, depression is the fulfilment of the death drive.

ESTHER: A fulfilment?

YEHUDA: Yes. Being more and more dead. That's why severe depression can lead to suicidal ideation.

ESTHER: That's why you said at the time that it's hard to treat depression, because you're treating someone who is not interested in their own lack; they have no lack to present to you.

YEHUDA: Yes.

ESTHER: That's why?

YEHUDA: Right, they aren't in a position to ask for anything. They lack for nothing.

ESTHER: But on the other hand, they are very demanding.

YEHUDA: The demanding part is the undepressed part; the part that still desires. When a person is severely depressed, even their demanding nature dimin-ishes. When they say, "I'll just lie here alone in the dark," they truly mean it. They aren't being manipulative.

ESTHER: I'll just lie here alone in the dark because I don't mind dying?

YEHUDA: Because I want to be in a place where I can no longer feel alive, because being alive is being in pain.

ESTHER: Precisely, that's what it is.

YEHUDA: And what else can we say about death? One of the finest solutions to death, in my opinion, is being eternal. We don't have to die! We can let the story in which we play a role go on after our physical death, to have a connection to something greater than our physical lives. Lacan says that the first death survives the second death. The first death occurs when words replace things. Even dogs, who are part of the human community, have this ability to enjoy a kind word instead of a treat. With people it's even clearer: most of the things we enjoy are symbolic. The symbol replaced the thing and can satisfy. Meaning, the first death occurs when the word replaces the thing. The first death survives the second death.

ESTHER: The first survives the second: even when you die, words survive you.

YEHUDA: Exactly. The words created in the first death, the death of the thing itself – those words don't die when the organism dies. The grave, the headstone, the heritage, the inheritance, the fact that people remember the dead – all these things are the symbolic existence that continues beyond the organic existence. The more a person identifies with their symbolic existence in their lives, the more eternal they are; the more they see themselves as something that isn't fixed in the organic body, but rather belongs to a different order. When you identify with a story that is larger than your life, you buy yourself a share of eternity. The subject that is sustained by making a message continues to exist as long as the message continues to be heard, even after organic death. Even without the credit, the memory, as long as the influence is perpetuated, death is not complete.

ESTHER: Lacan says, "The word killed the thing," not "replaced the thing," correct?

YEHUDA: Correct, correct. There is a phenomenon that Lacan referred to as "retroaction." Actions I take today receive meaning from what happens in the future. The simple approach would be: Jews kiss the mezuzah because God said so. The more complex approach would say: kissing a mezuzah is a way to create God. This is a reversal of cause and effect. The effect – meaning, the rituals – creates the cause, which is God. This is a reversal of cause and effect. You could take this principle and spread it across a timeline: rather than assume I'm doing something in the present in order to make something else happen in the future, I am fulfilling something in the present.

ESTHER: I'm fulfilling something in the present and by doing this I am validating the past, right? The past exists by virtue of the present. You tell the story of the past in the present, therefore validating it.

YEHUDA: There is a legend about the Jewish scholar Honi HaMe'agel, who met an old man planting carob trees. The trees would yield fruit only seventy years later, when the old man would no longer be alive. That means that the timeline the planter deemed relevant was not limited to his mortal life. He thus expanded his frame of reference beyond his organic life. The more important to you the things that take place after your death, the more eternal you are and the more connected to things beyond your life.

I'll say it again: we live in a myth either way. No matter what, we live in a story we tell ourselves. Can the story be broad and long enough so as not to end with our physical death? So that the actions we take now –

ESTHER: Can be taken knowing they would receive meaning in the future, after our deaths.

YEHUDA: Yes. Yes.

ESTHER: That this carob, someone would eat it –

YEHUDA: Right.

ESTHER: And that would be something that gives meaning to our existence as cause.

YEHUDA: Yes.

ESTHER: It's like we turn ourselves into the cause. Yes, we turn ourselves into a cause by planting a carob for the future, and then the cause exists by virtue of the effect. That's what you were trying to say before.

YEHUDA: Yes, yes.

ESTHER: By virtue of the carob eaten eighty years after my death, I exist as a cause.

YEHUDA: I plant myself inside the carob seed so that I can live there in the future.

ESTHER: Exactly. All right.

YEHUDA: And the broader in space and the longer in time the frame of reference is – in the Symbolic order – the longer the life with which I identify.

ESTHER: Yes.

YEHUDA: There's something else we do with death, which is using the moment of death, the thought of how I would feel about the life I had, as an acid test for desire. How do I know what I want, out of my variety of desires? By using "deathbed calculations." When I lie on my deathbed, thinking back to the dilemma I had today, which decision would I live peacefully with? That doesn't mean that's actually what I will think when death comes to take me, but it can be a compass connecting me to my desire today.

ESTHER: You're saying, "We have no choice but to live. We know little about death, so let's use it as a tool for life."

YEHUDA: Correct.

ESTHER: This is what we leave our readers with at the end of this chapter: Listen, there is an afterlife, there isn't an afterlife – that's all speculation. It's a metaphysics that depends on a theory into which it is woven. I'm putting it this way because that's what the Buddha said.

YEHUDA: Okay.

ESTHER: The Buddha denied metaphysical discussions of the afterlife – not metaphysics as a discipline, only the discussion of it. We disappear at some point. Some call it Nirvana; other people call it paradise, the afterlife. There are all sorts of names for it, but the only knowledge we have is that life as we know it is finite. It's something that ends. Since it is finite, let's use the knowledge of this finiteness in order to live.

YEHUDA: Now, there is a variation of the fear of death, which is the fear of those who remain and miss the dead. A person might fear death because of their sorrow for those who would mourn them.

ESTHER: The sorrow they cause others. That's a reason to avoid suicide. I think that's a real reason. It serves choice in many people's lives. But sometimes this reason falls out of the net. When the Symbolic net, the meaning a person grants their own life, can no longer hold it.

YEHUDA: Yes.

ESTHER: But when there is suicidal ideation, and alongside it a grip on life in the full sense of the phrase, then sometimes a person will avoid suicide simply because they don't want to upset others. Don't you think?

YEHUDA: The fact that you care how people will feel after your death means it isn't entirely "your death."

ESTHER: For example, if a person is very sick, they might make the choice not to go through a long and painful death. But they know that the early separation, which is a result of a choice, would be unbearable to their children, so they go through the entire path for their children. I think it's like that sometimes.

YEHUDA: I think sometimes there's a measure of delusion to it.

ESTHER: You do?

YEHUDA: And the foundation of the fraud is narcissistic. I want to flatter myself by thinking others won't make it without me.

ESTHER: That I'm so important. In this way, you don't take responsibility for your own will to live.

YEHUDA: Right, right. That's why if you tell a sick or suicidal person, "We'll miss you but eventually we'll be all right," it's an opportunity for them to say, "On second thought, I want to live."

ESTHER: Rather than take offense.

YEHUDA: That's right.

ESTHER: Hang on. You started from an interesting point. This is something I witnessed with my own eyes, and it got me thinking but also resisting. A person lies on their deathbed, and a pain doctor comes in to fix him a drug cocktail and says, "Let go, you can die." That's a concept in our culture: "You're free to leave, we're letting you go." Sometimes people say that to a dying relative.

YEHUDA: They set them free.

ESTHER: Yeah, they sort of "set them free." To me, that's awful.

YEHUDA: Yeah, but there is a liberation in it. You thought you had to suffer for us, but you don't have to. We'll be all right. There's a liberation in it. There can be.

ESTHER: To me, it's brash, you know? It's arrogant, to say that to a person on their deathbed. I was very upset when I heard a doctor say it. I think these things should be forbidden to say. They aren't right. We know nothing about death and very little about dying. In my experience, this is a situation we don't understand properly because it's difficult to understand. People in this situation are not fully communicative even when they are fully conscious. It's very interesting. I wrote a lot about that.

YEHUDA: Will you share it?

ESTHER: Dying seems to me like a very specific situation, very distinct from others, even though we are dying our entire lives, which is very clear to me. Buddhism can sometimes seem morbid, or look morbid from a distance, which is why in western thought Nirvana is perceived as a death wish. Because

Buddhism deals with preparations for death, but from an orientation of life, just as you said. Preparing for death truly means no longer fearing death, because fear of death is at the foundation of all fears. As far as I'm concerned, every fear is a fear of death. Fear of rejection is a fear of death. Fear of insult is a fear of death. In the west, we give our different kinds of fears lots of respect, dividing them into different types, but underneath them all lies one great fear, and that is the fear of dying. That's where it all starts. If someone insults you, you are afraid, quite simply, that you might die. It's the same fear. The volumes are different, the stories people tell themselves are different, but in truth, it's always the fear of not existing, of being erased, crumbled, crushed.

YEHUDA: A patient asks what is the right way to conduct herself in order not to lose her partner, and the answer is, prepare for separation. So she can lean on herself. That is the best way to preserve the relationship. I take this as a metaphor for our attitude toward death: living while preparing to die – living in the way that is best for life itself.

ESTHER: The Zen masters, the real, great Zen masters, die at a late age, and known when they're about to die. There's a poem they write before death. There's a collection Yoel Hoffman edited, called *Japanese Death Poems: Written by Zen Monks and Haiku Poets on the Verge of Death*. Every Zen master writes a poem of parting from life. It's an ancient, powerful custom. Things like, "I've had enough; I put down the chopsticks." There is therefore a basis for the thought that every person – not only these masters, for whom it is clear – performs an absolute act of renunciation, a final act of renunciation, which brings death at the end of dying. An act that is not entirely organic.

YEHUDA: Yes.

ESTHER: It would be easy to doubt my words when you think about how the final decision maker is the body. But the mind has a part in it, an act of renunciation. I talk about this out of the awareness that, at the end of life, a person must choose to die. In that sense, we mustn't "let them go." No one has the right to interfere with this decision.

YEHUDA: Yes.

ESTHER: It's sort of like how, in your clinic, you don't take the choice away from your patient. That is the most powerful rule for you as a clinician.

YEHUDA: Yes.

ESTHER: Not to take their choice away. Right?

YEHUDA: Right.

ESTHER: You're with them, you're beside them, you stay as close to them as possible, but you don't do it for them. So you can't tell them, "You can let go," either. You see?

YEHUDA: Yes.

ESTHER: Don't choose for them. I've clarified my position on this to myself.

YEHUDA: Okay. I've learned something new. Another subject related to what we said previously about using death to give meaning to life: life has two goals. One is to enjoy. The second is to do good in the world.

ESTHER: Who said that? It's interesting. It's real ethics.

YEHUDA: Most situations demand choosing one or the other. Lacan said that in all sorts of ways.

ESTHER: Did he?

YEHUDA: Yes. In the complex way that he said it, he borrowed concepts from Karl Marx – use value and exchange value. In goods, there can be use value or exchange value. You can consume goods or invest them, and then they will have exchange value, and their exchange value will go up. That's capitalism. Consuming goods is instant gratification, its pleasure, while exchanging or converting it, trading it – is delaying gratification. Delaying gratification is sacrificing your pleasure for something else – either for future pleasure or for the sake of others. If it's for future pleasure, we're back to choosing pleasure. If not, we're choosing to do something for the world. Now, I'm not saying what's the right thing to do, I'm just showing you the map. Those are, generally, the two options. In short, we call them *jouissance* and desire. *Jouissance* is the pleasure of satisfaction or excitement, of no-meaning, and desire is the pleasure of meaning. Desiring goes beyond death. If what's left after me is my effect on the world, if I generated change, if I planted a carob tree, that's the influence that remains after my death. The more I identify with my influences, the more infinite I am. But let's not confuse this with acknowledgement, with getting credit for planting the tree. This isn't what this is about. It's about the fact that the thing I created will exist. That's the influence, that's the way people continue to exist through their influences. Chassids call this a "pipe." We mentioned this before. Being a conduit, the object things pass through, brings up the question of how you change the things that pass through you in this world.

It's the end of the chapter and the end of the book. What can we say about endings in this context, talking about death and coming to the end?

ESTHER: That it's always a little sad, when something is lost. When something is over. Our pleasure in writing this book is over.

YEHUDA: Yes.

ESTHER: And to our readers, hopefully –

YEHUDA: This book is over.

ESTHER: The pleasure of reading it is over.

YEHUDA: Right.

ESTHER: Right? Sometimes people linger while reading a book . . . sometimes, when you find a good book, it's sad to finish reading it.

YEHUDA: Right. It's better to start a new book before finishing the old one.

ESTHER: So that's it. That's the story. And as always, words cannot cover the extent of the experience.

YEHUDA: So it ends with a whimper, no bombastic closing declarations.

ESTHER: They won't do us any good anyway . . .

YEHUDA: All right. So that's it, then. But desire is still around, is it not?

Index

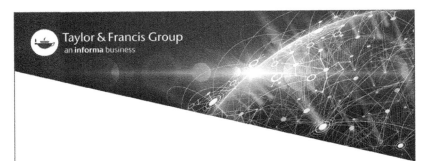

For Product Safety Concerns and Information please contact our EU
representative GPSR@taylorandfrancis.com Taylor & Francis Verlag GmbH,
Kaufingerstraße 24, 80331 München, Germany

Printed and bound by CPI Group (UK) Ltd, Croydon, CR0 4YY
08/06/2025
01896986-0017